Table of Contents

Chapter 1: Introduction

The Glorious Quran, the Word of God revealed to prophet Muhammad, contains a universal message to all mankind. A brief summary of the message of the Quran would read as follows:

There is no god but God, Lord of all the worlds. The guided ones believe in God and worship Him without associating anyone or anything with Him. God sends His messengers with the guidance and He sent prophet Muhammad to deliver the Quran. The Quran is the manual that explains and details Islam, and Islam (submission to God), is the means to attain Paradise in the Hereafter.

Any words in the Quran speak directly or indirectly about any of the statements above.

The comprehensive message of the Quran, as summarized above, cannot be found in its entirety in one Sura but is found in key sentences that are found all over the Quran. Except for a few locations where a complete story is told from beginning to end in one chapter, such as the story of Joseph in Sura 12, the Quran is not a collection of tales placed one next to the other. In addition, although the Quran contains many historical accounts of various people and times, the Quran is not intended to be a historical reference as such. Historic details in the Quran are not narrated for their historic merit, but because they serve the overall message of the Book.

It must also be pointed out that the selection of the key sentences on its own does not produce a comprehensive summary, but it is the deliberate placing of the sentences in a very specific order that yields a comprehensive presentation of the Quranic message in a naturally flowing manner.

Let us take the subject of Salat as an example. The rules and the details of the Salat cannot all be found in one Sura, but are spread over numerous Suras. The purpose of the Salat, most importantly the commemoration and glorification of God, is found in Sura 29 (verse 45) and Sura 20 (verse 14). The Qibla is mentioned in Sura 2 (verse 149), and the wudu' (ablution) is found in Sura 5 (verse 6). Various other details of the Salat are found in yet other Suras.

There are several reasons why the Quran does not present information in the same manner we would see in any other book. In any textbook, subjects start with an introduction. This is followed by the development of the subject and ends with a conclusion. One reason why the Quran does not follow the customary procedure is that the Quran is not a textbook, nor is it obliged to follow the literary rules that humans invented. A better description of the Quran is that it is a book containing

Numerical Design spells out the Quranic Message

———————————

By: A. S. Mohamed

Cover design: A. S. Mohamed
Page layout: Moshood Saliu

statements of truth. Statements of truth do not require specific presentations or sequential displays.

When we come to the key sentences presented in this search, it is important to note that not any sentences were used in the presentation, but only the sentences that satisfy the following guidelines:

1- Every sentence is a complete sentence. Many are only parts of verses, but each is a complete sentence.

2- Every sentence portrays a definite message.

3- Every sentence is an integral part of the overall message of the Quran.

The following examples demonstrate how many of these sentences are complete sentences even though they are not complete verses.

| Know that there is no god but God | 47:19 | اَعْلَمْ أَنَّهُۥ لَآ إِلَٰهَ إِلَّا ٱللَّهُ |
| God has selected the religion for you | 2:132 | إِنَّ ٱللَّهَ ٱصْطَفَىٰ لَكُمُ ٱلدِّينَ |

The number of key sentences presented in this search exceeds 600 sentences and they are connected by one common attribute as will be seen.

As for the sequence of sentences, which is derived from various Suras of the Quran, the following five sentences provide an example of this feature:

And God created you, then He takes you back	16:70	وَٱللَّهُ خَلَقَكُمْ ثُمَّ يَتَوَفَّىٰكُمْ
God takes back the selves at the time of their death	39:42	يَتَوَفَّى ٱلْأَنفُسَ حِينَ مَوْتِهَا
We inherit the earth and all who are on it	19:40	نَحْنُ نَرِثُ ٱلْأَرْضَ وَمَنْ عَلَيْهَا
The One who initiated you from a single self	6:98	ٱلَّذِىٓ أَنشَأَكُم مِّن نَّفْسٍ وَٰحِدَةٍ
Then behold, you are human beings spreading out	30:20	ثُمَّ إِذَآ أَنتُم بَشَرٌ تَنتَشِرُونَ

As is evident, the five sentences above are taken from five different Suras of the Quran. However, when they are placed in the above sequence, the outcome is in perfect harmony with the overall Quranic message.

For demonstration purposes, the large number of those key sentences required that they be grouped by subject as follows:

1- God: The First and The Last, Creator and Sustainer of the Universe.

2- Messenger: Sent by God to deliver the Quran.

3- Quran: A beacon for the righteous and a manual of Islam.

4- Islam: The religion authorised by God.

5- Hereafter: Following Islam is the means for redemption in the Hereafter.

Important note

It is important to note that the sentences presented in the coming chapters are not intended to be a substitute or a re-arrangement of the Holy Quran in any way. They merely serve to portray the message of the Quran and offer a better understanding of its divine message.

Chapter 2: God

As with any of the previous Scriptures revealed by God, the prime message of the Quran is the proclamation of the existence of God, that there is no god other than He, and that He has absolute authority and sovereignty over all that is in the Heavens and the Earth.

God created the Heavens and the Earth, the seven universes and the Sun and the Moon. God created everything on Earth including the human being. Significant details are given in the Quran about the creation of the human being.

Besides the creation of the Earth, God ordained everything in the Earth and the sea to be subservient to man. God provided man from the Earth and the sky in measured amounts.

To God belongs the unseen of the Heavens and the Earth and God is Knowledgeable of all things. He is the One who brings to life and puts to death, and to Him, all shall be returned. Indeed, to God belongs the inheritance of the Heavens and the Earth.

God is the Light of the Heavens and the Earth, and He guides to His light whom He wills.

God is Seer and Knowledgeable of what people do, and God is Knowledgeable of what the chests hold.

God has immense mercy and forgiveness for the people despite their transgressions, and He is the Forgiver of sins. God is Possessor of great favour for the people.

God declared that it is binding on Him to support the believers; God never breaks a promise.

God is Rich, Praiseworthy, Knowledgeable and Wise.

God is Merciful, Forgiver, Pardoner and the Redeemer.

God is Gentle, All-Aware and Dignified.

God is Hearer, Seer and Capable of all things.

Such is God our Lord; it is Him alone whom we should worship.

The following Quranic sentences provide a more detailed account of the above information:

God

The First and The Last, Creator and Sustainer of the Universe

1	Indeed I am God, Lord of the Worlds	28:30	إِنِّى أَنَا ٱللَّهُ رَبُّ ٱلْعَٰلَمِينَ
2	Know that there is no god except God	47:19	ٱعْلَمْ أَنَّهُۥ لَآ إِلَٰهَ إِلَّا ٱللَّهُ
3	The Almighty: He settled on the Throne	20:5	ٱلرَّحْمَٰنُ عَلَى ٱلْعَرْشِ ٱسْتَوَىٰ
4	Worship Me, for that is a straight path	36:61	ٱعْبُدُونِى هَٰذَا صِرَٰطٌ مُّسْتَقِيمٌ
5	The One who created seven universes in layers	67:3	ٱلَّذِى خَلَقَ سَبْعَ سَمَٰوَٰتٍ طِبَاقًا
6	We built above you seven mighty ones	78:12	بَنَيْنَا فَوْقَكُمْ سَبْعًا شِدَادًا
7	And We guarded it against every outcast devil	15:17	وَحَفِظْنَٰهَا مِن كُلِّ شَيْطَٰنٍ رَّجِيمٍ
8	God created the heavens and the earth	45:22	خَلَقَ ٱللَّهُ ٱلسَّمَٰوَٰتِ وَٱلْأَرْضَ
9	And the sun runs along to its place of settlement	36:38	وَٱلشَّمْسُ تَجْرِى لِمُسْتَقَرٍّ لَّهَا
10	He has set for them a specified term about which there is no doubt	17:99	وَجَعَلَ لَهُمْ أَجَلًا لَّا رَيْبَ فِيهِ
11	And that is easy for God	4:30	وَكَانَ ذَٰلِكَ عَلَى ٱللَّهِ يَسِيرًا
12	And God created you and what you make	37:96	وَٱللَّهُ خَلَقَكُمْ وَمَا تَعْمَلُونَ
13	He created and fashioned, and the One who proportioned and guided	87:2-3	خَلَقَ فَسَوَّىٰ وَٱلَّذِى قَدَّرَ فَهَدَىٰ

14	And God created you, then He takes you back	16:70	وَٱللَّهُ خَلَقَكُمْ ثُمَّ يَتَوَفَّىٰكُمْ
15	God takes back the selves at the time of their death	39:42	يَتَوَفَّى ٱلْأَنفُسَ حِينَ مَوْتِهَا
16	We inherit the earth and all who are on it	19:40	نَحْنُ نَرِثُ ٱلْأَرْضَ وَمَنْ عَلَيْهَا
17	The One who initiated you from a single self	6:98	ٱلَّذِىٓ أَنشَأَكُم مِّن نَّفْسٍ وَٰحِدَةٍ
18	Then behold, you are human beings spreading out	30:20	ثُمَّ إِذَآ أَنتُم بَشَرٌ تَنتَشِرُونَ
19	Whomever We grant a long life, We decline him in stature	36:68	مَن نُّعَمِّرْهُ نُنَكِّسْهُ فِى ٱلْخَلْقِ
20	He created the human being. He taught him the art of expression	55:3-4	خَلَقَ ٱلْإِنسَٰنَ عَلَّمَهُ ٱلْبَيَانَ
21	Carrying him and weaning him takes thirty months	46:15	وَحَمْلُهُۥ وَفِصَٰلُهُۥ ثَلَٰثُونَ شَهْرًا
22	We created you from a male and female	49:13	إِنَّا خَلَقْنَٰكُم مِّن ذَكَرٍ وَأُنثَىٰ
23	He has made for you spouses from among yourselves	42:11	جَعَلَ لَكُم مِّنْ أَنفُسِكُمْ أَزْوَٰجًا
24	The One who created death and life	67:2	ٱلَّذِى خَلَقَ ٱلْمَوْتَ وَٱلْحَيَوٰةَ
25	so that He may test you as to whose work is better	67:2	لِيَبْلُوَكُمْ أَيُّكُمْ أَحْسَنُ عَمَلًا
26	The One who rendered the earth a cradle for you	20:53	ٱلَّذِى جَعَلَ لَكُمُ ٱلْأَرْضَ مَهْدًا

27	You thread wide paths therein	71:20	تَسْلُكُوا۟ مِنْهَا سُبُلًا فِجَاجًا
28	The One who rendered the earth a habitat for you	2:22	ٱلَّذِى جَعَلَ لَكُمُ ٱلْأَرْضَ فِرَٰشًا
29	And He placed stabilisers therein that rise above it	41:10	وَجَعَلَ فِيهَا رَوَٰسِىَ مِن فَوْقِهَا
30	And He brought water down for you from the sky	27:60	وَأَنزَلَ لَكُم مِّنَ ٱلسَّمَآءِ مَآءً
31	Whereby He brings to life the land after it has died	45:5	أَحْيَا بِهِ ٱلْأَرْضَ بَعْدَ مَوْتِهَا
32	Then with it, We produce all kinds of fruits	7:57	فَأَخْرَجْنَا بِهِۦ مِن كُلِّ ٱلثَّمَرَٰتِ
33	He shows you the lightning, striking fear as well as inspiring hope	30:24	يُرِيكُمُ ٱلْبَرْقَ خَوْفًا وَطَمَعًا
34	And among His signs are the night and the day	41:37	وَمِنْ ءَايَٰتِهِ ٱلَّيْلُ وَٱلنَّهَارُ
35	And due to Him is the alternation of the night and day	23:80	وَلَهُ ٱخْتِلَٰفُ ٱلَّيْلِ وَٱلنَّهَارِ
36	Indeed, in that are signs for the knowledgeable	30:22	إِنَّ فِى ذَٰلِكَ لَءَايَٰتٍ لِّلْعَٰلِمِينَ
37	He created everything and proportioned it with utmost precision	25:2	خَلَقَ كُلَّ شَىْءٍ فَقَدَّرَهُۥ تَقْدِيرًا
38	He created the jinn from a fusion of fire	55:15	خَلَقَ ٱلْجَآنَّ مِن مَّارِجٍ مِّن نَّارٍ
39	God created every creature from water	24:45	وَٱللَّهُ خَلَقَ كُلَّ دَآبَّةٍ مِّن مَّآءٍ

40	We made from water all living things	21:30	جَعَلْنَا مِنَ ٱلْمَآءِ كُلَّ شَىْءٍ حَىٍّ
41	God has set for everything its measure	65:3	قَدْ جَعَلَ ٱللَّهُ لِكُلِّ شَىْءٍ قَدْرًا
42	To God belongs what is in the heavens and the earth	24:64	لِلَّهِ مَا فِى ٱلسَّمَٰوَٰتِ وَٱلْأَرْضِ
43	And to Him belongs all who are in the heavens and the earth	21:19	وَلَهُۥ مَن فِى ٱلسَّمَٰوَٰتِ وَٱلْأَرْضِ
44	To God belongs the inheritance of the heavens and the earth	3:180	لِلَّهِ مِيرَٰثُ ٱلسَّمَٰوَٰتِ وَٱلْأَرْضِ
45	And to God belongs the sovereignty of the heavens and the earth	3:189	وَلِلَّهِ مُلْكُ ٱلسَّمَٰوَٰتِ وَٱلْأَرْضِ
46	And God grants His sovereignty to whom He wills	2:247	وَٱللَّهُ يُؤْتِى مُلْكَهُۥ مَن يَشَآءُ
47	To God belong the soldiers of the heavens and the earth	48:4	لِلَّهِ جُنُودُ ٱلسَّمَٰوَٰتِ وَٱلْأَرْضِ
48	And none knows the soldiers of your Lord except Him	74:31	وَمَا يَعْلَمُ جُنُودَ رَبِّكَ إِلَّا هُوَ
49	He knows the unseen of the heavens and the earth	49:18	يَعْلَمُ غَيْبَ ٱلسَّمَٰوَٰتِ وَٱلْأَرْضِ
50	And to God belongs the unseen of the heavens and the earth	11:123	وَلِلَّهِ غَيْبُ ٱلسَّمَٰوَٰتِ وَٱلْأَرْضِ
51	He knows what is declared and what is hidden	87:7	إِنَّهُۥ يَعْلَمُ ٱلْجَهْرَ وَمَا يَخْفَىٰ

52	And He knows what is in the land and the sea	6:59	وَيَعْلَمُ مَا فِى ٱلْبَرِّ وَٱلْبَحْرِ
53	And God is Knowledgeable of all things	33:40	وَكَانَ ٱللَّهُ بِكُلِّ شَىْءٍ عَلِيمًا
54	And He is the One who takes you back during the night	6:60	وَهُوَ ٱلَّذِى يَتَوَفَّىٰكُم بِٱلَّيْلِ
55	And He knows what you have done during the day	6:60	وَيَعْلَمُ مَا جَرَحْتُم بِٱلنَّهَارِ
56	He is the Truth, and He brings the dead to life	22:6	هُوَ ٱلْحَقُّ وَأَنَّهُ يُحْىِ ٱلْمَوْتَىٰ
57	He brings to life and puts to death, and to Him you shall be returned	10:56	يُحْىِ وَيُمِيتُ وَإِلَيْهِ تُرْجَعُونَ
58	We bring to life and put to death, and We are the Inheritors	15:23	نُحْىِ وَنُمِيتُ وَنَحْنُ ٱلْوَٰرِثُونَ
59	God is Capable to do that	4:133	وَكَانَ ٱللَّهُ عَلَىٰ ذَٰلِكَ قَدِيرًا
60	You will find that there is no substitute for the Sunna of God	35:43	لَن تَجِدَ لِسُنَّتِ ٱللَّهِ تَبْدِيلًا
61	You will find that there is no diversion from the Sunna of God	35:43	لَن تَجِدَ لِسُنَّتِ ٱللَّهِ تَحْوِيلًا
62	So blessed be God, the Lord of the Worlds	40:64	فَتَبَارَكَ ٱللَّهُ رَبُّ ٱلْعَٰلَمِينَ
63	The Provider, the Possessor of Power, the Robust	51:58	ٱلرَّزَّاقُ ذُو ٱلْقُوَّةِ ٱلْمَتِينُ

64	They said, "The Almighty has taken unto Himself a son"	19:88	قَالُوا۟ ٱتَّخَذَ ٱلرَّحْمَـٰنُ وَلَدًا
65	It is not for God to take a son	19:35	مَا كَانَ لِلَّهِ أَن يَتَّخِذَ مِن وَلَدٍ
66	The heavens almost shatter from it	19:90	تَكَادُ ٱلسَّمَـٰوَٰتُ يَتَفَطَّرْنَ مِنْهُ
67	Glory to Him and exalted is He, far above what they say	17:43	سُبْحَـٰنَهُۥ وَتَعَـٰلَىٰ عَمَّا يَقُولُونَ
68	Glory to Him and exalted is He, far above what they associate with Him	30:40	سُبْحَـٰنَهُۥ وَتَعَـٰلَىٰ عَمَّا يُشْرِكُونَ
69	They assign daughters to God, Glory to Him	16:57	يَجْعَلُونَ لِلَّهِ ٱلْبَنَـٰتِ سُبْحَـٰنَهُۥ
70	You should know that God is Rich, Praiseworthy	2:267	ٱعْلَمُوٓا۟ أَنَّ ٱللَّهَ غَنِىٌّ حَمِيدٌ
71	And He does not have a partner in the sovereignty	25:2	وَلَمْ يَكُن لَّهُۥ شَرِيكٌ فِى ٱلْمُلْكِ
72	And that God is the Most High, the Great	31:30	أَنَّ ٱللَّهَ هُوَ ٱلْعَلِىُّ ٱلْكَبِيرُ
73	Indeed, God is beyond need of all the worlds	29:6	إِنَّ ٱللَّهَ لَغَنِىٌّ عَنِ ٱلْعَـٰلَمِينَ
74	God is the Light of the heavens and the earth	24:35	ٱللَّهُ نُورُ ٱلسَّمَـٰوَٰتِ وَٱلْأَرْضِ
75	God guides to His Light whom He wills	24:35	يَهْدِى ٱللَّهُ لِنُورِهِۦ مَن يَشَآءُ
76	Victory comes only from God	8:10	مَا ٱلنَّصْرُ إِلَّا مِنْ عِندِ ٱللَّهِ
77	God supports with His victory whom He wills	3:13	ٱللَّهُ يُؤَيِّدُ بِنَصْرِهِۦ مَن يَشَآءُ

78	It is binding on Us to support the believers	30:47	حَقًّا عَلَيْنَا نَصْرُ ٱلْمُؤْمِنِينَ
79	So do not think that God would break His promise	14:47	لَا تَحْسَبَنَّ ٱللَّهَ مُخْلِفَ وَعْدِهِ
80	God never breaks a promise	3:9	إِنَّ ٱللَّهَ لَا يُخْلِفُ ٱلْمِيعَادَ
81	Your Lord suffices as a Guide and a Supporter	25:31	وَكَفَىٰ بِرَبِّكَ هَادِيًا وَنَصِيرًا
82	Indeed, nothing is hidden from God	3:5	إِنَّ ٱللَّهَ لَا يَخْفَىٰ عَلَيْهِ شَىْءٌ
83	Your Lord is not unaware of what you do	27:93	وَمَا رَبُّكَ بِغَٰفِلٍ عَمَّا تَعْمَلُونَ
84	God is Witness over what you do	3:98	ٱللَّهُ شَهِيدٌ عَلَىٰ مَا تَعْمَلُونَ
85	Your Lord is Most Knowledgeable of what is within yourselves	17:25	رَبُّكُمْ أَعْلَمُ بِمَا فِى نُفُوسِكُمْ
86	And God is Knowledgeable of what the chests hold	64:4	وَٱللَّهُ عَلِيمٌ بِذَاتِ ٱلصُّدُورِ
87	Indeed, God is All Aware of what you do	59:18	إِنَّ ٱللَّهَ خَبِيرٌ بِمَا تَعْمَلُونَ
88	Indeed, God is Watchful over you	4:1	إِنَّ ٱللَّهَ كَانَ عَلَيْكُمْ رَقِيبًا
89	Indeed, God is Knowledgeable of what they do	35:8	إِنَّ ٱللَّهَ عَلِيمٌ بِمَا يَصْنَعُونَ
90	God encompasses what they do	3:120	إِنَّ ٱللَّهَ بِمَا يَعْمَلُونَ مُحِيطٌ
91	God wishes to redeem you	4:27	ٱللَّهُ يُرِيدُ أَن يَتُوبَ عَلَيْكُمْ

92	And indeed, your Lord has forgiveness for the people	13:6	وَإِنَّ رَبَّكَ لَذُو مَغْفِرَةٍ لِّلنَّاسِ
93	Who forgives the sins except for God?	3:135	مَن يَغْفِرُ ٱلذُّنُوبَ إِلَّا ٱللَّهُ
94	God forgives all sins	39:53	ٱللَّهَ يَغْفِرُ ٱلذُّنُوبَ جَمِيعًا
95	The Forgiver of sins and the Acceptor of repentance	40:3	غَافِرِ ٱلذَّنْبِ وَقَابِلِ ٱلتَّوْبِ
96	You grant dignity to whom You will, and You humiliate whom You will	3:26	تُعِزُّ مَن تَشَآءُ وَتُذِلُّ مَن تَشَآءُ
97	And You provide for whom You please without count	3:27	وَتَرْزُقُ مَن تَشَآءُ بِغَيْرِ حِسَابٍ
98	Indeed, your Lord is Possessor of Favour for the people	27:73	إِنَّ رَبَّكَ لَذُو فَضْلٍ عَلَى ٱلنَّاسِ
99	God is Possessor of Favour for all the worlds	2:251	ٱللَّهَ ذُو فَضْلٍ عَلَى ٱلْعَٰلَمِينَ
100	And what God brings down from the sky	45:5	وَمَآ أَنزَلَ ٱللَّهُ مِنَ ٱلسَّمَآءِ
101	He brings down to you provisions from the sky	40:13	يُنَزِّلُ لَكُم مِّنَ ٱلسَّمَآءِ رِزْقًا
102	We do not bring it down except in a known measure	15:21	مَا نُنَزِّلُهُۥٓ إِلَّا بِقَدَرٍ مَّعْلُومٍ
103	Your Lord extends the provision to whom He wills	17:30	رَبَّكَ يَبْسُطُ ٱلرِّزْقَ لِمَن يَشَآءُ
104	God showers His blessings on whom He wills of His servants	14:11	يَمُنُّ عَلَىٰ مَن يَشَآءُ مِنْ عِبَادِهِ
105	This is indeed a clear favour	27:16	إِنَّ هَٰذَا لَهُوَ ٱلْفَضْلُ ٱلْمُبِينُ

106	And indeed, God is Compassionate and Merciful towards you	57:9	وَإِنَّ ٱللَّهَ بِكُمْ لَرَءُوفٌ رَّحِيمٌ
107	Then indeed, He is Forgiver towards the repentant ones	17:25	فَإِنَّهُ كَانَ لِلْأَوَّٰبِينَ غَفُورًا
108	He sends the winds which then stir up clouds	30:48	يُرْسِلُ ٱلرِّيَٰحَ فَتُثِيرُ سَحَابًا
109	And so you see the rain coming out from within it	30:48	فَتَرَى ٱلْوَدْقَ يَخْرُجُ مِنْ خِلَٰلِهِ
110	The One who brought water down from the sky	6:99	ٱلَّذِيٓ أَنزَلَ مِنَ ٱلسَّمَآءِ مَآءً
111	He darkened its night and brought out its brightness	79:29	أَغْطَشَ لَيْلَهَا وَأَخْرَجَ ضُحَٰهَا
112	Take a look at the effects of God's mercy	30:50	ٱنظُرْ إِلَىٰٓ ءَاثَٰرِ رَحْمَتِ ٱللَّهِ
113	How He brings the land to life after it had died	30:50	كَيْفَ يُحْىِ ٱلْأَرْضَ بَعْدَ مَوْتِهَا
114	And We placed therein gardens of palm trees	36:34	وَجَعَلْنَا فِيهَا جَنَّٰتٍ مِّن نَّخِيلٍ
115	God thus cites the examples	13:17	كَذَٰلِكَ يَضْرِبُ ٱللَّهُ ٱلْأَمْثَالَ
116	The mercy of your Lord is better than whatever they can amass	43:32	رَحْمَتُ رَبِّكَ خَيْرٌ مِّمَّا يَجْمَعُونَ
117	The donation of your Lord is never restricted	17:20	وَمَا كَانَ عَطَآءُ رَبِّكَ مَحْظُورًا
118	God has subjected for you what is in the earth	22:65	ٱللَّهَ سَخَّرَ لَكُم مَّا فِى ٱلْأَرْضِ
119	God is the One who subjected the sea for you	45:12	ٱللَّهُ ٱلَّذِى سَخَّرَ لَكُمُ ٱلْبَحْرَ

120	There are signs in the earth for those with certainty	51:20	فِى ٱلْأَرْضِ ءَايَٰتٌ لِّلْمُوقِنِينَ
121	And also in yourselves. Can you not see?	51:21	وَفِىٓ أَنفُسِكُمْ أَفَلَا تُبْصِرُونَ
122	Whichever sign We instate or cause to be forgotten	2:106	مَا نَنسَخْ مِنْ ءَايَةٍ أَوْ نُنسِهَا
123	Say, "The signs are only with God	29:50	قُلْ إِنَّمَا ٱلْءَايَٰتُ عِندَ ٱللَّهِ
124	Praise be to God. He will show you His signs	27:93	ٱلْحَمْدُ لِلَّهِ سَيُرِيكُمْ ءَايَٰتِهِ
125	God cites for the people their examples	47:3	يَضْرِبُ ٱللَّهُ لِلنَّاسِ أَمْثَٰلَهُمْ
126	But none understand them except the knowledgeable	29:43	وَمَا يَعْقِلُهَآ إِلَّا ٱلْعَٰلِمُونَ
127	So do not cite the examples to God	16:74	فَلَا تَضْرِبُوا۟ لِلَّهِ ٱلْأَمْثَالَ
128	God alternates the night and the day	24:44	يُقَلِّبُ ٱللَّهُ ٱلَّيْلَ وَٱلنَّهَارَ
129	Which of your Lord's favours do you deny	55:18	بِأَىِّ ءَالَآءِ رَبِّكُمَا تُكَذِّبَانِ
130	God is the Master of those who believe	47:11	ٱللَّهَ مَوْلَى ٱلَّذِينَ ءَامَنُوا۟
131	While the disbelievers have no master	47:11	وَأَنَّ ٱلْكَٰفِرِينَ لَا مَوْلَىٰ لَهُمْ
132	God is not unjust towards the servants	8:51	أَنَّ ٱللَّهَ لَيْسَ بِظَلَّٰمٍ لِّلْعَبِيدِ
133	Indeed, your Lord will judge between them in accordance with His Law	27:78	إِنَّ رَبَّكَ يَقْضِى بَيْنَهُم بِحُكْمِهِ

134	We have created the human being into hardship	90:4	لَقَدْ خَلَقْنَا ٱلْإِنسَـٰنَ فِى كَبَدٍ
135	We do not assign to any self except what is within its capacity	23:62	وَلَا نُكَلِّفُ نَفْسًا إِلَّا وُسْعَهَا
136	God will follow difficulty with ease	65:7	سَيَجْعَلُ ٱللَّهُ بَعْدَ عُسْرٍ يُسْرًا
137	He will not deprive you of any of your deeds	49:14	لَا يَلِتْكُم مِّنْ أَعْمَـٰلِكُمْ شَيْـًٔا
138	Indeed, God is the Rich and Praiseworthy One	57:24	إِنَّ ٱللَّهَ هُوَ ٱلْغَنِىُّ ٱلْحَمِيدُ
139	Indeed, God is Knowledgeable, Wise	4:11	إِنَّ ٱللَّهَ كَانَ عَلِيمًا حَكِيمًا
140	Indeed, God is Redeemer, Merciful	4:16	إِنَّ ٱللَّهَ كَانَ تَوَّابًا رَّحِيمًا
141	Indeed, God is Forgiver, Merciful	4:23	إِنَّ ٱللَّهَ كَانَ غَفُورًا رَّحِيمًا
142	Indeed, God is Knowledgeable, All Aware	4:35	إِنَّ ٱللَّهَ كَانَ عَلِيمًا خَبِيرًا
143	Indeed, God is Gentle, All Aware	33:34	إِنَّ ٱللَّهَ كَانَ لَطِيفًا خَبِيرًا
144	Indeed, God is Dignified, Wise	4:56	إِنَّ ٱللَّهَ كَانَ عَزِيزًا حَكِيمًا
145	Indeed, God is Hearer, Seer	4:58	إِنَّ ٱللَّهَ كَانَ سَمِيعًا بَصِيرًا
146	Then indeed, God is Pardoner, Capable	4:149	فَإِنَّ ٱللَّهَ كَانَ عَفُوًّا قَدِيرًا

147	Judgment belongs to Him, and to Him you shall be returned	28:70	وَلَهُ ٱلْحُكْمُ وَإِلَيْهِ تُرْجَعُونَ
148	Such is God your Lord. To Him belongs the sovereignty	35:13	ذَلِكُمُ ٱللَّهُ رَبُّكُمْ لَهُ ٱلْمُلْكُ
149	Such is God your Lord, so worship Him	10:3	ذَلِكُمُ ٱللَّهُ رَبُّكُمْ فَٱعْبُدُوهُ

Chapter 3: The Messenger

God, exalted is He, does not come down to man, rather, God sends His messengers with the guidance. They are sent to deliver God's Message. Indeed, the sole duty of the messenger is to deliver God's Message (5:99).

And since the people receive God's message through the human messenger, it is the duty of all believers to obey God and His messenger.

God sent prophet Muhammad, the seal of all the prophets to the world to deliver the Quran.

The Holy Ruh (Gabriel) brought down the Holy Quran to prophet Muhammad. In turn, God's messenger was commanded to follow what was revealed to him by His lord and to hold fast to it.

The messenger is commanded to preach to the people the worship of God alone and the importance of devoting the religion purely to God alone.

If the people deny the messenger, he is to leave them alone, for he is not a guardian nor a trustee over them. Those who deny God's messengers shall be the losers in the Hereafter.

God supports His messengers and He granted prophet Muhammad a great victory.

The messenger of God will never ask people for a reward for his work. His work is but a notification and a Message from God.

The following Quranic sentences provide a more detailed account of the above information:

The Messenger

Sent by God to deliver the Quran

1	We have sent to you a messenger	73:15	إِنَّآ أَرْسَلْنَآ إِلَيْكُمْ رَسُولًا
2	We sent a messenger to you from amongst you	2:151	أَرْسَلْنَا فِيكُمْ رَسُولًا مِّنكُمْ
3	And to teach you the Scripture and wisdom	2:151	وَيُعَلِّمُكُمُ ٱلْكِتَـٰبَ وَٱلْحِكْمَةَ
4	The messenger of God and the seal of the prophets	33:40	رَّسُولَ ٱللَّهِ وَخَاتَمَ ٱلنَّبِيِّـۧنَ
5	Say "Obey God and the messenger"	3:32	قُلْ أَطِيعُواْ ٱللَّهَ وَٱلرَّسُولَ
6	The sole duty of the messenger is the delivery	5:99	مَّا عَلَى ٱلرَّسُولِ إِلَّا ٱلْبَلَـٰغُ
7	God is my Lord and your Lord, so worship Him	3:51	ٱللَّهَ رَبِّى وَرَبُّكُمْ فَٱعْبُدُوهُ
8	We have sent messengers before you	13:38	لَقَدْ أَرْسَلْنَا رُسُلًا مِّن قَبْلِكَ
9	And We granted them wives and offspring	13:38	وَجَعَلْنَا لَهُمْ أَزْوَٰجًا وَذُرِّيَّةً
10	They do not intercede except for those whom He is pleased with	21:28	لَا يَشْفَعُونَ إِلَّا لِمَنِ ٱرْتَضَىٰ
11	God chooses for Himself whom He wills	42:13	ٱللَّهُ يَجْتَبِى إِلَيْهِ مَن يَشَآءُ
12	Those who deliver God's messages	33:39	ٱلَّذِينَ يُبَلِّغُونَ رِسَـٰلَـٰتِ ٱللَّهِ
13	He brings down to His servant clear revelations	57:9	يُنَزِّلُ عَلَىٰ عَبْدِهِۦ ءَايَـٰتٍۭ بَيِّنَـٰتٍ

14	Thus, We have brought down to you the Book	29:47	كَذَٰلِكَ أَنزَلْنَآ إِلَيْكَ ٱلْكِتَٰبَ
15	Say "The Holy Ruh has brought it down from your Lord"	16:102	قُلْ نَزَّلَهُۥ رُوحُ ٱلْقُدُسِ مِن رَّبِّكَ
16	He brought it down upon your heart with God's permission	2:97	نَزَّلَهُۥ عَلَىٰ قَلْبِكَ بِإِذْنِ ٱللَّهِ
17	And We have given you a Reminder from Us	20:99	وَقَدْ ءَاتَيْنَٰكَ مِن لَّدُنَّا ذِكْرًا
18	You can only warn the one who follows the Reminder	36:11	إِنَّمَا تُنذِرُ مَنِ ٱتَّبَعَ ٱلذِّكْرَ
19	So give him good news of forgiveness and a generous reward	36:11	فَبَشِّرْهُ بِمَغْفِرَةٍ وَأَجْرٍ كَرِيمٍ
20	Follow what is being revealed to you from your Lord	33:2	ٱتَّبِعْ مَا يُوحَىٰٓ إِلَيْكَ مِن رَّبِّكَ
21	Hold fast to what has been revealed to you	43:43	ٱسْتَمْسِكْ بِٱلَّذِىٓ أُوحِىَ إِلَيْكَ
22	And do not be an advocate for the betrayers	4:105	وَلَا تَكُن لِّلْخَآئِنِينَ خَصِيمًا
23	O you prophet, strive against the disbelievers	66:9	يَٰٓأَيُّهَا ٱلنَّبِىُّ جَٰهِدِ ٱلْكُفَّارَ
24	Indeed, God does not like the disbelievers	3:32	فَإِنَّ ٱللَّهَ لَا يُحِبُّ ٱلْكَٰفِرِينَ
25	Do not be distressed by what they scheme	27:70	لَا تَكُن فِى ضَيْقٍ مِّمَّا يَمْكُرُونَ
26	Messengers before you were ridiculed	6:10	لَقَدِ ٱسْتُهْزِئَ بِرُسُلٍ مِّن قَبْلِكَ

27	You are not, by the blessing of your Lord, a madman	68:2	مَآ أَنتَ بِنِعْمَةِ رَبِّكَ بِمَجْنُونٍ
28	Say, "I have been commanded to worship God	39:11	قُلْ إِنِّىٓ أُمِرْتُ أَنْ أَعْبُدَ ٱللَّهَ
29	God is the One I worship, devoting my religion purely to Him	39:14	ٱللَّهَ أَعْبُدُ مُخْلِصًا لَّهُۥ دِينِى
30	So go on worshipping what you please besides Him	39:15	فَٱعْبُدُوا۟ مَا شِئْتُم مِّن دُونِهِۦ
31	You will surely be questioned about what you used to do	16:93	لَتُسْـَٔلُنَّ عَمَّا كُنتُمْ تَعْمَلُونَ
32	So turn away from them, for you are not to be blamed	51:54	فَتَوَلَّ عَنْهُمْ فَمَآ أَنتَ بِمَلُومٍ
33	Then leave them playing in their vain discourse	6:91	ثُمَّ ذَرْهُمْ فِى خَوْضِهِمْ يَلْعَبُونَ
34	In the Hereafter, they will be the greatest losers	11:22	فِى ٱلْـَٔاخِرَةِ هُمُ ٱلْأَخْسَرُونَ
35	We did not send you as a guardian over them	4:80	فَمَآ أَرْسَلْنَـٰكَ عَلَيْهِمْ حَفِيظًا
36	We did not send you as a trustee over them	17:54	وَمَآ أَرْسَلْنَـٰكَ عَلَيْهِمْ وَكِيلًا
37	Their reckoning is in no way your responsibility	6:52	مَا عَلَيْكَ مِنْ حِسَابِهِم مِّن شَىْءٍ
38	Your sole duty is the clear delivery	16:82	إِنَّمَا عَلَيْكَ ٱلْبَلَـٰغُ ٱلْمُبِينُ
39	God's favour upon you is great	4:113	كَانَ فَضْلُ ٱللَّهِ عَلَيْكَ عَظِيمًا

40	Indeed, We have granted you a clear conquest	48:1	إِنَّا فَتَحْنَا لَكَ فَتْحًا مُّبِينًا
41	And God supports you with an honourable victory	48:3	وَيَنصُرَكَ ٱللَّهُ نَصْرًا عَزِيزًا
42	Say "I do not ask you for a reward for it"	25:57	قُلْ مَآ أَسْـَٔلُكُم عَلَيْهِ مِنْ أَجْرٍ
43	I am a warner and bearer of good news from Him to you	11:2	إِنَّنِى لَكُم مِّنْهُ نَذِيرٌ وَبَشِيرٌ
44	I possess no power to harm you, nor to guide you	72:21	لَآ أَمْلِكُ لَكُمْ ضَرًّا وَلَا رَشَدًا
45	It is but a notification from God, and His messages	72:23	إِلَّا بَلَٰغًا مِّنَ ٱللَّهِ وَرِسَٰلَٰتِهِ
46	God bears witness by what He has brought down to you	4:166	ٱللَّهُ يَشْهَدُ بِمَآ أَنزَلَ إِلَيْكَ
47	And say, "The truth has arrived, and the falsehood has perished"	17:81	وَقُلْ جَآءَ ٱلْحَقُّ وَزَهَقَ ٱلْبَٰطِلُ
48	What is there after the truth except for misguidance?	10:32	مَاذَا بَعْدَ ٱلْحَقِّ إِلَّا ٱلضَّلَٰلُ

Chapter 4: The Quran

The Quran, a revelation from God to mankind, was brought down as an Arabic Quran. The Quran contains clear revelations and harbours no crookedness. None disbelieves in the Quranic revelations except those with sickness in their hearts and the wicked.

The Quran is indeed a Reminder and it provides guidance and healing for the believers.

God guides with the Quran whom He wills, and it is the believers who obey God and follow what God revealed.

The Quran is fully detailed. It contains a detailed account of all things and is made easy for the remembrance. Indeed, the Word of God is complete in truth and justice.

The following Quranic sentences provide a more detailed account of the above information:

The Quran

A Beacon for the righteous and a manual of Islam

#			
1	In the name of God, the Almighty, the Merciful	1:1	بِسْمِ ٱللَّهِ ٱلرَّحْمَٰنِ ٱلرَّحِيمِ
2	A revelation from the Almighty, the Merciful	41:2	تَنزِيلٌ مِّنَ ٱلرَّحْمَٰنِ ٱلرَّحِيمِ
3	He is the One who brought down upon you the Book	3:7	هُوَ ٱلَّذِىٓ أَنزَلَ عَلَيْكَ ٱلْكِتَٰبَ
4	A Noble Quran in a well-protected Book	56:77-78	قُرْءَانٌ كَرِيمٌ فِى كِتَٰبٍ مَّكْنُونٍ
5	A Glorious Quran in a Preserved Tablet	85:21-22	قُرْءَانٌ مَّجِيدٌ فِى لَوْحٍ مَّحْفُوظٍ
6	There is no doubt about it; it is from the Lord of the Worlds	10:37	لَا رَيْبَ فِيهِ مِن رَّبِّ ٱلْعَٰلَمِينَ
7	We have brought it down as an Arabic Quran	12:2	إِنَّآ أَنزَلْنَٰهُ قُرْءَانًا عَرَبِيًّا
8	An Arabic Quran without any crookedness	39:28	قُرْءَانًا عَرَبِيًّا غَيْرَ ذِى عِوَجٍ
9	We thus brought it down as a law in Arabic	13:37	كَذَٰلِكَ أَنزَلْنَٰهُ حُكْمًا عَرَبِيًّا
10	And thus, We have brought it down in the form of clear revelations	22:16	وَكَذَٰلِكَ أَنزَلْنَٰهُ ءَايَٰتٍ بَيِّنَٰتٍ
11	None disbelieves in them except the wicked	2:99	مَا يَكْفُرُ بِهَآ إِلَّا ٱلْفَٰسِقُونَ
12	For those who believe, it is guidance and healing	41:44	لِلَّذِينَ ءَامَنُوا۟ هُدًى وَشِفَآءٌ

13	Blessed is the One who brought down the Criterion	25:1	تَبَارَكَ ٱلَّذِى نَزَّلَ ٱلْفُرْقَانَ
14	God has brought down to you a Reminder	65:10	قَدْ أَنزَلَ ٱللَّهُ إِلَيْكُمْ ذِكْرًا
15	And advice and a reminder for the believers	11:120	وَمَوْعِظَةٌ وَذِكْرَىٰ لِلْمُؤْمِنِينَ
16	And guidance and mercy for people who are certain	45:20	وَهُدًى وَرَحْمَةٌ لِّقَوْمٍ يُوقِنُونَ
17	There is a notification in this for a worshipping people	21:106	فِى هَٰذَا لَبَلَٰغًا لِّقَوْمٍ عَٰبِدِينَ
18	That they may know that He is but One God	14:52	لِيَعْلَمُوٓاْ أَنَّمَا هُوَ إِلَٰهٌ وَٰحِدٌ
19	Advice has come to you from your Lord	10:57	قَدْ جَآءَتْكُم مَّوْعِظَةٌ مِّن رَّبِّكُمْ
20	And guidance and mercy for people who believe	16:64	وَهُدًى وَرَحْمَةً لِّقَوْمٍ يُؤْمِنُونَ
21	He guides with it whom He wills of His servants	6:88	يَهْدِى بِهِۦ مَن يَشَآءُ مِنْ عِبَادِهِۦ
22	And indeed, it is a revelation from the Lord of the Worlds	26:192	وَإِنَّهُۥ لَتَنزِيلُ رَبِّ ٱلْعَٰلَمِينَ
23	Follow what has been revealed to you from your Lord	6:106	ٱتَّبِعْ مَآ أُوحِىَ إِلَيْكَ مِن رَّبِّكَ
24	He brought down to you the Book fully detailed	6:114	أَنزَلَ إِلَيْكُمُ ٱلْكِتَٰبَ مُفَصَّلًا
25	A detailed account of all things, and guidance and mercy	12:111	تَفْصِيلَ كُلِّ شَىْءٍ وَهُدًى وَرَحْمَةً
26	Mercy and a reminder for people who believe	29:51	رَحْمَةً وَذِكْرَىٰ لِقَوْمٍ يُؤْمِنُونَ

27	We did not leave anything out of the Book	6:38	مَّا فَرَّطْنَا فِى ٱلْكِتَـٰبِ مِن شَىْءٍ
28	We made the Quran easy for the remembrance	54:17	قَدْ يَسَّرْنَا ٱلْقُرْءَانَ لِلذِّكْرِ
29	Then, when We recite it, follow its recitation	75:18	إِذَا قَرَأْنَـٰهُ فَٱتَّبِعْ قُرْءَانَهُ
30	The Word of your Lord has been completed, in truth and justice	6:115	تَمَّتْ كَلِمَتُ رَبِّكَ صِدْقًا وَعَدْلًا

Chapter 5: Islam

Islam (submission to God) is the religion prescribed by God for mankind. It is fully detailed in the Quran. To be a Muslim is to submit to God's absolute authority, to worship God alone, and to obey God's commandments. Genuine submitters to God are those who devote their religion totally and purely to God alone, never associating partners with God in any capacity.

The do's and do nots of Islam are detailed in the Book of God. Reverence, righteousness and the upholding of the worship rituals are integral acts of Islam.

Those who believe in God's messengers and uphold the articles of Islam are promised Paradise and its great rewards. Those who disbelieve in God and His messengers, who were sent to them with the proofs, are warned of a great punishment in Hell.

God knows the contents of the hearts and is Seer of all people. Those who fabricate lies about God and those who conceal the truth of God are promised a great punishment. The same goes for those who indulge in all kinds of sin, spreading corruption in the land. Those are allowed a little enjoyment in their worldly life then they are destined for great punishment.

Clear warnings are given not to follow the footsteps of the devil who is a clear enemy of the human being. The devil will adorn sinful acts in the eyes of people and will entice them to disbelieve and commit all kinds of wickedness and corruption.

Observing the Salat, giving the Zakat, as well as the other articles of Islam are all components of the religion that God decreed for mankind.

During a person's lifetime and before the time when death comes, the door of repentance is left open by God. Not only does God accept the repentance of His servants and forgive all their sins but as a sign of His infinite mercy and generosity, God replaces the bad deeds of those who repent and reform into good deeds.

The following Quranic sentences provide a more detailed account of the above information:

Islam

The religion authorised by God

1	God has selected the religion for you	2:132	إِنَّ ٱللَّهَ ٱصْطَفَىٰ لَكُمُ ٱلدِّينَ
2	So worship Him. This is a straight path	3:51	فَٱعْبُدُوهُ هَٰذَا صِرَٰطٌ مُّسْتَقِيمٌ
3	Worship your Lord who created you	2:21	ٱعْبُدُوا۟ رَبَّكُمُ ٱلَّذِى خَلَقَكُمْ
4	Direct your face towards the religion as a monotheist	10:105	أَنْ أَقِمْ وَجْهَكَ لِلدِّينِ حَنِيفًا
5	And call upon Him, devoting the religion purely to Him	7:29	وَٱدْعُوهُ مُخْلِصِينَ لَهُ ٱلدِّينَ
6	O people, reverence your Lord	31:33	يَٰٓأَيُّهَا ٱلنَّاسُ ٱتَّقُوا۟ رَبَّكُمْ
7	Who sent His messenger with the guidance	48:28	ٱلَّذِىٓ أَرْسَلَ رَسُولَهُۥ بِٱلْهُدَىٰ
8	Peace be upon the one who follows the guidance	20:47	ٱلسَّلَٰمُ عَلَىٰ مَنِ ٱتَّبَعَ ٱلْهُدَىٰ
9	Do not call upon another god besides God	28:88	لَا تَدْعُ مَعَ ٱللَّهِ إِلَٰهًا ءَاخَرَ
10	Devoted to God alone, associating none with Him	22:31	حُنَفَآءَ لِلَّهِ غَيْرَ مُشْرِكِينَ بِهِ
11	And warn your close relatives	26:214	وَأَنذِرْ عَشِيرَتَكَ ٱلْأَقْرَبِينَ
12	So call upon Him, devoting the religion purely to Him	40:65	فَٱدْعُوهُ مُخْلِصِينَ لَهُ ٱلدِّينَ

13	And reverence Him and observe the Salat	30:31	وَٱتَّقُوهُ وَأَقِيمُوا۟ ٱلصَّلَوٰةَ
14	And do not be of those who associate partners with God	30:31	وَلَا تَكُونُوا۟ مِنَ ٱلْمُشْرِكِينَ
15	They will be repaid for what they used to do	7:180	سَيُجْزَوْنَ مَا كَانُوا۟ يَعْمَلُونَ
16	We have prepared for them a painful punishment	17:10	أَعْتَدْنَا لَهُمْ عَذَابًا أَلِيمًا
17	Indeed, in that is a lesson for those who fear	79:26	إِنَّ فِى ذَلِكَ لَعِبْرَةً لِّمَن يَخْشَىٰ
18	But the hypocrites do not know	63:8	لَـٰكِنَّ ٱلْمُنَـٰفِقِينَ لَا يَعْلَمُونَ
19	Do not be a supporter of the disbelievers	28:86	لَا تَكُونَنَّ ظَهِيرًا لِّلْكَـٰفِرِينَ
20	The ones who disbelieved in God's revelations	39:63	ٱلَّذِينَ كَفَرُوا۟ بِـَٔايَـٰتِ ٱللَّهِ
21	They disbelieved in what has come to you of the truth	60:1	كَفَرُوا۟ بِمَا جَآءَكُم مِّنَ ٱلْحَقِّ
22	After the guidance became clear to them	47:25	مِّنۢ بَعْدِ مَا تَبَيَّنَ لَهُمُ ٱلْهُدَى
23	But those who disbelieved are in denial	85:19	بَلِ ٱلَّذِينَ كَفَرُوا۟ فِى تَكْذِيبٍ
24	They are, at the mention of the Almighty, disbelievers.	21:36	هُم بِذِكْرِ ٱلرَّحْمَـٰنِ هُمْ كَـٰفِرُونَ
25	What is the matter with you that you do not believe in God	57:8	وَمَا لَكُمْ لَا تُؤْمِنُونَ بِٱللَّهِ
26	When God alone was called upon you disbelieved	40:12	إِذَا دُعِىَ ٱللَّهُ وَحْدَهُ كَفَرْتُمْ

27	As fuel for Hell; you will surely come to it	21:98	حَصَبُ جَهَنَّمَ أَنتُمْ لَهَا وَارِدُونَ
28	Be patient, and patience is attainable only with God's help	16:127	أصْبِرْ وَمَا صَبْرُكَ إِلَّا بِٱللَّهِ
29	And do not be distressed by what they scheme	16:127	وَلَا تَكُ فِى ضَيْقٍ مِّمَّا يَمْكُرُونَ
30	Stay away from the one who turned away from Our remembrance	53:29	أَعْرِضْ عَن مَّن تَوَلَّىٰ عَن ذِكْرِنَا
31	For us are our deeds, and for you are your deeds	42:15	لَنَآ أَعْمَـٰلُنَا وَلَكُمْ أَعْمَـٰلُكُمْ
32	The guidance has come to them from their Lord	53:23	لَقَدْ جَآءَهُم مِّن رَّبِّهِمُ ٱلْهُدَىٰ
33	And their messengers came to them with the clear proofs	10:13	وَجَآءَتْهُمْ رُسُلُهُم بِٱلْبَيِّنَـٰتِ
34	But they placed their hands in their mouths and said	14:9	فَرَدُّوٓاْ أَيْدِيَهُمْ فِىٓ أَفْوَٰهِهِمْ
35	Indeed, we have disbelieved in what you have been sent with	14:9	إِنَّا كَفَرْنَا بِمَآ أُرْسِلْتُم بِهِ
36	But the hypocrites do not understand	63:7	لَـٰكِنَّ ٱلْمُنَـٰفِقِينَ لَا يَفْقَهُونَ
37	They have ears with which they do not hear	7:179	لَهُمْ ءَاذَانٌ لَّا يَسْمَعُونَ بِهَآ
38	These are like cattle. In fact, they are further astray	7:179	أُوْلَـٰٓئِكَ كَٱلْأَنْعَـٰمِ بَلْ هُمْ أَضَلُّ
39	God knows best what is in their hearts	11:31	ٱللَّهُ أَعْلَمُ بِمَا فِىٓ أَنفُسِهِمْ

32

40	They have turned arrogant in themselves	25:21	لَقَدِ ٱسْتَكْبَرُوا۟ فِىٓ أَنفُسِهِمْ
41	Most of them follow nothing but conjecture	10:36	وَمَا يَتَّبِعُ أَكْثَرُهُمْ إِلَّا ظَنًّا
42	God knows their secrets and their private conferring	9:78	ٱللَّهَ يَعْلَمُ سِرَّهُمْ وَنَجْوَىٰهُمْ
43	There is not much good in most of their private conferring	4:114	لَّا خَيْرَ فِى كَثِيرٍ مِّن نَّجْوَىٰهُمْ
44	They confer to commit sin and transgression	58:8	يَتَنَٰجَوْنَ بِٱلْإِثْمِ وَٱلْعُدْوَٰنِ
45	They are plotting some scheme, and I am plotting a scheme	86:15-16	يَكِيدُونَ كَيْدًا وَأَكِيدُ كَيْدًا
46	We have tested those before them	29:3	لَقَدْ فَتَنَّا ٱلَّذِينَ مِن قَبْلِهِمْ
47	And how many a generation We have annihilated before them	50:36	وَكَمْ أَهْلَكْنَا قَبْلَهُم مِّن قَرْنٍ
48	They denied and followed their personal desires	54:3	كَذَّبُوا۟ وَٱتَّبَعُوٓا۟ أَهْوَآءَهُمْ
49	And they say lies about God	3:75	وَيَقُولُونَ عَلَى ٱللَّهِ ٱلْكَذِبَ
50	Who is more transgressing than one who lies about God	39:32	مَنْ أَظْلَمُ مِمَّن كَذَبَ عَلَى ٱللَّهِ
51	He is the one who will roast in the greatest Fire	87:12	ٱلَّذِى يَصْلَى ٱلنَّارَ ٱلْكُبْرَىٰ
52	Then he will neither die in it nor live	87:13	ثُمَّ لَا يَمُوتُ فِيهَا وَلَا يَحْيَىٰ

53	But God has cursed them for their disbelief	4:46	وَلَٰكِن لَّعَنَهُمُ ٱللَّهُ بِكُفْرِهِم
54	And We have placed veils over their hearts	17:46	وَجَعَلْنَا عَلَىٰ قُلُوبِهِمْ أَكِنَّةً
55	This is because they are a people who do not understand	59:13	ذَٰلِكَ بِأَنَّهُمْ قَوْمٌ لَّا يَفْقَهُونَ
56	This is because they are people who do not reason	59:14	ذَٰلِكَ بِأَنَّهُمْ قَوْمٌ لَّا يَعْقِلُونَ
57	This is because they are a people who do not know	9:6	ذَٰلِكَ بِأَنَّهُمْ قَوْمٌ لَّا يَعْلَمُونَ
58	So leave them in their confusion until a certain time	23:54	فَذَرْهُمْ فِى غَمْرَتِهِمْ حَتَّىٰ حِينٍ
59	And We have already known those who progress	15:24	وَلَقَدْ عَلِمْنَا ٱلْمُسْتَقْدِمِينَ
60	And We have already known those who regress	15:24	وَلَقَدْ عَلِمْنَا ٱلْمُسْتَـْٔخِرِينَ
61	God dislikes every ungrateful sinner	2:276	ٱللَّهُ لَا يُحِبُّ كُلَّ كَفَّارٍ أَثِيمٍ
62	He lets them extend their transgression as they blunder blindly	2:15	يَمُدُّهُمْ فِى طُغْيَٰنِهِمْ يَعْمَهُونَ
63	A little enjoyment, then they shall have a painful punishment	16:117	مَتَٰعٌ قَلِيلٌ وَلَهُمْ عَذَابٌ أَلِيمٌ
64	The excessive ones are the companions of the Fire	40:43	ٱلْمُسْرِفِينَ هُمْ أَصْحَٰبُ ٱلنَّارِ
65	A little enjoyment, then their refuge is Hell	3:197	مَتَٰعٌ قَلِيلٌ ثُمَّ مَأْوَىٰهُمْ جَهَنَّمُ

66	But He respites them until a specified term	16:61	لَـٰكِن يُؤَخِّرُهُمْ إِلَىٰ أَجَلٍ مُّسَمًّى
67	And their selves will depart while they are disbelievers	9:85	وَتَزْهَقَ أَنفُسُهُمْ وَهُمْ كَـٰفِرُونَ
68	And the Word is rightly deserved upon the disbelievers	36:70	وَيَحِقَّ ٱلْقَوْلُ عَلَى ٱلْكَـٰفِرِينَ
69	Ah! Indeed, the disbelievers never succeed	28:82	وَيْكَأَنَّهُۥ لَا يُفْلِحُ ٱلْكَـٰفِرُونَ
70	And the disbelievers shall have a severe punishment	42:26	وَٱلْكَـٰفِرُونَ لَهُمْ عَذَابٌ شَدِيدٌ
71	They will be arraigned unto the punishment	34:38	أُوْلَـٰئِكَ فِى ٱلْعَذَابِ مُحْضَرُونَ
72	And We will let them taste some of the harsh punishment	41:50	وَلَنُذِيقَنَّهُم مِّنْ عَذَابٍ غَلِيظٍ
73	We prepared for them the punishment of the Blaze	67:5	أَعْتَدْنَا لَهُمْ عَذَابَ ٱلسَّعِيرِ
74	Do not follow the footsteps of the devil	2:168	وَلَا تَتَّبِعُواْ خُطُوَٰتِ ٱلشَّيْطَـٰنِ
75	The devil is disobedient to the Almighty	19:44	ٱلشَّيْطَـٰنَ كَانَ لِلرَّحْمَـٰنِ عَصِيًّا
76	The devil is a clear enemy to the human being	12:5	ٱلشَّيْطَـٰنَ لِلْإِنسَـٰنِ عَدُوٌّ مُّبِينٌ
77	And the devil adorned their works for them	27:24	وَزَيَّنَ لَهُمُ ٱلشَّيْطَـٰنُ أَعْمَـٰلَهُمْ
78	And the devil is ever ungrateful to his Lord	17:27	وَكَانَ ٱلشَّيْطَـٰنُ لِرَبِّهِۦ كَفُورًا

79	Indeed, the devil's scheming is weak	4:76	إِنَّ كَيْدَ ٱلشَّيْطَٰنِ كَانَ ضَعِيفًا
80	Do not let the Deceiver delude you about God	31:33	لَا يَغُرَّنَّكُم بِٱللَّهِ ٱلْغَرُورُ
81	So seek provisions from God	29:17	فَٱبْتَغُوا۟ عِندَ ٱللَّهِ ٱلرِّزْقَ
82	And give thanks to Him. To Him, you shall be returned	29:17	وَٱشْكُرُوا۟ لَهُۥٓ إِلَيْهِ تُرْجَعُونَ
83	Whoever is ungrateful, then indeed, God is Rich, Praiseworthy	31:12	مَن كَفَرَ فَإِنَّ ٱللَّهَ غَنِيٌّ حَمِيدٌ
84	Pilgrimage to the House is a duty owed to God by the people	3:97	وَلِلَّهِ عَلَى ٱلنَّاسِ حِجُّ ٱلْبَيْتِ
85	Complete the Hajj and Umrah for God	2:196	وَأَتِمُّوا۟ ٱلْحَجَّ وَٱلْعُمْرَةَ لِلَّهِ
86	And strive in the cause of God with the striving that is due to Him	22:78	وَجَٰهِدُوا۟ فِى ٱللَّهِ حَقَّ جِهَادِهِ
87	And do not confuse the truth with falsehood	2:42	وَلَا تَلْبِسُوا۟ ٱلْحَقَّ بِٱلْبَٰطِلِ
88	But most of you hate the truth	43:78	وَلَٰكِنَّ أَكْثَرَكُمْ لِلْحَقِّ كَٰرِهُونَ
89	Call upon your Lord humbly and privately	7:55	ٱدْعُوا۟ رَبَّكُمْ تَضَرُّعًا وَخُفْيَةً
90	Ask Him for forgiveness, then repent to Him	11:61	ٱسْتَغْفِرُوهُ ثُمَّ تُوبُوٓا۟ إِلَيْهِ
91	He accepts the repentance from His servants	9:104	هُوَ يَقْبَلُ ٱلتَّوْبَةَ عَنْ عِبَادِهِ

92	And will grant you a light with which you may walk	57:28	وَيَجْعَل لَّكُمْ نُورًا تَمْشُونَ بِهِ
93	And do not despair of God's grace	12:87	وَلَا تَايْـَٔسُوا۟ مِن رَّوْحِ ٱللَّهِ
94	Our Lord, grant us a mercy from You	18:10	رَبَّنَآ ءَاتِنَا مِن لَّدُنكَ رَحْمَةً
95	Or do they possess the treasuries of your Lord's mercy	38:9	أَمْ عِندَهُمْ خَزَآئِنُ رَحْمَةِ رَبِّكَ
96	Our Lord, avert from us the punishment of Hell	25:65	رَبَّنَا ٱصْرِفْ عَنَّا عَذَابَ جَهَنَّمَ
97	You alone we worship and You alone we ask for help	1:5	إِيَّاكَ نَعْبُدُ وَإِيَّاكَ نَسْتَعِينُ
98	Show us our worship rituals, and redeem us	2:128	أَرِنَا مَنَاسِكَنَا وَتُبْ عَلَيْنَآ
99	Our Lord, and make us Submitters to You	2:128	رَبَّنَا وَٱجْعَلْنَا مُسْلِمَيْنِ لَكَ
100	And grant us from You a supporter	4:75	وَٱجْعَل لَّنَا مِن لَّدُنكَ نَصِيرًا
101	God suffices us, He is the best Trustee	3:173	حَسْبُنَا ٱللَّهُ وَنِعْمَ ٱلْوَكِيلُ
102	The best Master and the best Supporter	22:78	نِعْمَ ٱلْمَوْلَىٰ وَنِعْمَ ٱلنَّصِيرُ
103	Remember God frequently	33:41	ٱذْكُرُوا۟ ٱللَّهَ ذِكْرًا كَثِيرًا
104	Absolutely, through the remembrance of God do the hearts feel assured	13:28	بِذِكْرِ ٱللَّهِ تَطْمَئِنُّ ٱلْقُلُوبُ
105	Yet they turn away from the remembrance of their Lord	21:42	بَلْ هُمْ عَن ذِكْرِ رَبِّهِم مُّعْرِضُونَ

106	Deaf, dumb and blind! Thus, they will not revert	2:18	صُمٌّ بُكْمٌ عُمْىٌ فَهُمْ لَا يَرْجِعُونَ
107	Indeed, those love the fleeting life	76:27	إِنَّ هَٰؤُلَآءِ يُحِبُّونَ ٱلْعَاجِلَةَ
108	And of the Hereafter, they are totally oblivious	30:7	وَهُمْ عَنِ ٱلْءَاخِرَةِ هُمْ غَٰفِلُونَ
109	So reverence God as best as you can	64:16	فَٱتَّقُواْ ٱللَّهَ مَا ٱسْتَطَعْتُمْ
110	And abstain from what is apparent of sin and what is concealed thereof	6:120	وَذَرُواْ ظَٰهِرَ ٱلْإِثْمِ وَبَاطِنَهُ
111	Put your trust in the Dignified, the Merciful	26:217	تَوَكَّلْ عَلَى ٱلْعَزِيزِ ٱلرَّحِيمِ
112	Observe the Salat at the two ends of the day	11:114	أَقِمِ ٱلصَّلَوٰةَ طَرَفِ ٱلنَّهَارِ
113	Observe the Salat at the duluk of the sun	17:78	أَقِمِ ٱلصَّلَوٰةَ لِدُلُوكِ ٱلشَّمْسِ
114	Take along your zinat to every masjid	7:31	خُذُواْ زِينَتَكُمْ عِندَ كُلِّ مَسْجِدٍ
115	Masjids where the name of God is mentioned	22:40	مَسَٰجِدُ يُذْكَرُ فِيهَا ٱسْمُ ٱللَّهِ
116	Give from the good that you have earned	2:267	أَنفِقُواْ مِن طَيِّبَٰتِ مَا كَسَبْتُمْ
117	And give the full measure and weight	6:152	وَأَوْفُواْ ٱلْكَيْلَ وَٱلْمِيزَانَ
118	God will enrich you from His favour	9:28	سَوْفَ يُغْنِيكُمُ ٱللَّهُ مِن فَضْلِهِ

119	Remember God's blessings upon you	33:9	ٱذۡكُرُواْ نِعۡمَةَ ٱللَّهِ عَلَيۡكُمۡ
120	Whatever blessing you have, it is from God	16:53	وَمَا بِكُم مِّن نِّعۡمَةٍ فَمِنَ ٱللَّهِ
121	My Lord extends the provision to whom He wills	34:36	رَبِّي يَبۡسُطُ ٱلرِّزۡقَ لِمَن يَشَآءُ
122	And He raised some of you above others in rank	6:165	وَرَفَعَ بَعۡضَكُمۡ فَوۡقَ بَعۡضٍ دَرَجَٰتٍ
123	My Ally is God, the One who brought down the Book	7:196	وَلِيِّيَ ٱللَّهُ ٱلَّذِى نَزَّلَ ٱلۡكِتَٰبَ
124	My Lord, enable me to give thanks for Your blessings	27:19	رَبِّ أَوۡزِعۡنِيٓ أَنۡ أَشۡكُرَ نِعۡمَتَكَ
125	My Lord, grant me a blessed disembarkation	23:29	رَّبِّ أَنزِلۡنِي مُنزَلًا مُّبَارَكًا
126	Indeed, We thus reward the good-doers	37:80	إِنَّا كَذَٰلِكَ نَجۡزِى ٱلۡمُحۡسِنِينَ
127	They avert a bad deed with a good deed	13:22	يَدۡرَءُونَ بِٱلۡحَسَنَةِ ٱلسَّيِّئَةَ
128	And they do not mix their faith with transgression	6:82	وَلَمۡ يَلۡبِسُوٓاْ إِيمَٰنَهُم بِظُلۡمٍ
129	Those are the ones whom God has guided	39:18	أُوْلَٰٓئِكَ ٱلَّذِينَ هَدَىٰهُمُ ٱللَّهُ
130	And those are the ones who possess intelligence	39:18	وَأُوْلَٰٓئِكَ هُمۡ أُوْلُواْ ٱلۡأَلۡبَٰبِ
131	We do not let the reward of those who do good works go to waste	18:30	لَا نُضِيعُ أَجۡرَ مَنۡ أَحۡسَنَ عَمَلًا

132	Whoever volunteers extra good work it is better for him	2:184	فَمَن تَطَوَّعَ خَيْرًا فَهُوَ خَيْرٌ لَّهُ
133	Do good as God has been good to you	28:77	أَحْسِن كَمَآ أَحْسَنَ ٱللَّهُ إِلَيْكَ
134	And lend God a good loan	73:20	وَأَقْرِضُوا۟ ٱللَّهَ قَرْضًا حَسَنًا
135	And do not forget your share of this world	28:77	وَلَا تَنسَ نَصِيبَكَ مِنَ ٱلدُّنْيَا
136	And do not seek corruption in the land	28:77	وَلَا تَبْغِ ٱلْفَسَادَ فِى ٱلْأَرْضِ
137	God is Knowledgeable of the corruptors	3:63	إِنَّ ٱللَّهَ عَلِيمٌۢ بِٱلْمُفْسِدِينَ
138	They do not give except begrudgingly	9:54	لَا يُنفِقُونَ إِلَّا وَهُمْ كَـٰرِهُونَ
139	Indeed, God does not like the corruptors	28:77	إِنَّ ٱللَّهَ لَا يُحِبُّ ٱلْمُفْسِدِينَ
140	Indeed, God does not like the aggressors	2:190	إِنَّ ٱللَّهَ لَا يُحِبُّ ٱلْمُعْتَدِينَ
141	Indeed, the transgressors are in an everlasting punishment	42:45	إِنَّ ٱلظَّـٰلِمِينَ فِى عَذَابٍ مُّقِيمٍ
142	No aggression is permitted except against the transgressors	2:193	لَا عُدْوَٰنَ إِلَّا عَلَى ٱلظَّـٰلِمِينَ
143	God dislikes every ungrateful betrayer	22:38	ٱللَّهَ لَا يُحِبُّ كُلَّ خَوَّانٍ كَفُورٍ
144	Indeed, God does not like the betrayers	8:58	إِنَّ ٱللَّهَ لَا يُحِبُّ ٱلْخَآئِنِينَ

145	God is Witness over what they do	10:46	ٱللَّهُ شَهِيدٌ عَلَىٰ مَا يَفْعَلُونَ
146	Indeed, God is Powerful, severe in punishment	8:52	إِنَّ ٱللَّهَ قَوِيٌّ شَدِيدُ ٱلْعِقَابِ
147	The punishment of the Hereafter is more severe and longer lasting	20:127	عَذَابُ ٱلْآخِرَةِ أَشَدُّ وَأَبْقَىٰ
148	Say, "Is that better, or the eternal Paradise"	25:15	قُلْ أَذَٰلِكَ خَيْرٌ أَمْ جَنَّةُ ٱلْخُلْدِ
149	So take heed, O you who possess vision	59:2	فَٱعْتَبِرُوا۟ يَٰأُو۟لِى ٱلْأَبْصَٰرِ
150	God is not unaware of what you do	3:99	مَا ٱللَّهُ بِغَٰفِلٍ عَمَّا تَعْمَلُونَ
151	Our messengers are writing down what you scheme	10:21	رُسُلَنَا يَكْتُبُونَ مَا تَمْكُرُونَ
152	Indeed, God is Seer of what you do	2:110	إِنَّ ٱللَّهَ بِمَا تَعْمَلُونَ بَصِيرٌ
153	And God encompasses all things	4:126	وَكَانَ ٱللَّهُ بِكُلِّ شَىْءٍ مُّحِيطًا
154	The bad and the good are not the same	5:100	لَّا يَسْتَوِى ٱلْخَبِيثُ وَٱلطَّيِّبُ
155	By your Lord, We will question them all	15:92	فَوَرَبِّكَ لَنَسْـَٔلَنَّهُمْ أَجْمَعِينَ
156	God will surely repay every self for what it has earned	14:51	يَجْزِىَ ٱللَّهُ كُلَّ نَفْسٍ مَّا كَسَبَتْ
157	The human being has nothing to count for him except his own work	53:39	أَن لَّيْسَ لِلْإِنسَٰنِ إِلَّا مَا سَعَىٰ

158	And then he will be repaid for it with the fullest reward	53:41	ثُمَّ يُجْزَىٰهُ ٱلْجَزَآءَ ٱلْأَوْفَىٰ
159	Every self earns for none other than itself	6:164	لَا تَكْسِبُ كُلُّ نَفْسٍ إِلَّا عَلَيْهَا
160	The self is indeed an enjoiner of sin	12:53	إِنَّ ٱلنَّفْسَ لَأَمَّارَةٌ بِٱلسُّوٓءِ
161	He inspired it with its depravity and its reverence	91:8	أَلْهَمَهَا فُجُورَهَا وَتَقْوَىٰهَا
162	He who strives, strives but for himself	29:6	مَن جَٰهَدَ فَإِنَّمَا يُجَٰهِدُ لِنَفْسِهِ
163	God does not wrong the people in any way	10:44	ٱللَّهَ لَا يَظْلِمُ ٱلنَّاسَ شَيْئًا
164	Whoever holds fast to God has been guided	3:101	وَمَن يَعْتَصِم بِٱللَّهِ فَقَدْ هُدِىَ
165	God bestows favour upon you by guiding you	49:17	ٱللَّهُ يَمُنُّ عَلَيْكُمْ أَنْ هَدَىٰكُمْ
166	The one whom God guides is the truly guided one	7:178	مَن يَهْدِ ٱللَّهُ فَهُوَ ٱلْمُهْتَدِى
167	And for those who are guided, He increases their guidance	47:17	وَٱلَّذِينَ ٱهْتَدَوْا۟ زَادَهُمْ هُدًى
168	Whomever God guides, none can misguide him	39:37	مَن يَهْدِ ٱللَّهُ فَمَا لَهُ مِن مُّضِلٍّ
169	As for those who disbelieved, for them is misery	47:8	وَٱلَّذِينَ كَفَرُوا۟ فَتَعْسًا لَّهُمْ
170	Have you seen the one who has taken his personal desire as his god?	25:43	أَرَءَيْتَ مَنِ ٱتَّخَذَ إِلَٰهَهُۥ هَوَىٰهُ

171	Hell is appropriate for him; what a miserable resting place	2:206	حَسْبُهُۥ جَهَنَّمُ وَلَبِئْسَ ٱلْمِهَادُ
172	Indeed, the criminals are in misguidance and sheer madness	54:47	إِنَّ ٱلْمُجْرِمِينَ فِى ضَلَٰلٍ وَسُعُرٍ
173	And they kill the prophets unjustly	3:21	وَيَقْتُلُونَ ٱلنَّبِيِّـۧنَ بِغَيْرِ حَقٍّ
174	Whomever God misguides, he will have no guide	7:186	مَن يُضْلِلِ ٱللَّهُ فَلَا هَادِىَ لَهُ
175	He leaves them blundering blindly in their transgression	7:186	يَذَرُهُمْ فِى طُغْيَٰنِهِمْ يَعْمَهُونَ
176	Until the Hour comes upon them suddenly	22:55	حَتَّىٰ تَأْتِيَهُمُ ٱلسَّاعَةُ بَغْتَةً
177	Or there comes to them the punishment of a barren day	22:55	أَوْ يَأْتِيَهُمْ عَذَابُ يَوْمٍ عَقِيمٍ
178	Until they see the painful punishment	10:97	حَتَّىٰ يَرَوُاْ ٱلْعَذَابَ ٱلْأَلِيمَ
179	And indeed, for the disbelievers is the punishment of the Fire	8:14	وَأَنَّ لِلْكَٰفِرِينَ عَذَابَ ٱلنَّارِ
180	Therein they shall permanently remain. What a miserable destination	64:10	خَٰلِدِينَ فِيهَا وَبِئْسَ ٱلْمَصِيرُ
181	Do not expend yourself in regret over them	35:8	لَا تَذْهَبْ نَفْسُكَ عَلَيْهِمْ حَسَرَٰتٍ
182	That has been inscribed in the Book	17:58	كَانَ ذَٰلِكَ فِى ٱلْكِتَٰبِ مَسْطُورًا
183	Indeed, this is in the earlier Scrolls	87:18	إِنَّ هَٰذَا لَفِى ٱلصُّحُفِ ٱلْأُولَىٰ

184	God purges those who believe	3:141	يُمَحِّصَ ٱللَّهُ ٱلَّذِينَ ءَامَنُوا۟
185	And whoever believes in God, He guides his heart	64:11	وَمَن يُؤْمِنۢ بِٱللَّهِ يَهْدِ قَلْبَهُ
186	God has bestowed favour upon the believers	3:164	قَدْ مَنَّ ٱللَّهُ عَلَى ٱلْمُؤْمِنِينَ
187	He will admit them into mercy from Him and favour	4:175	يُدْخِلُهُمْ فِى رَحْمَةٍ مِّنْهُ وَفَضْلٍ
188	And guides them to a straight path	5:16	وَيَهْدِيهِمْ إِلَىٰ صِرَٰطٍ مُّسْتَقِيمٍ
189	Indeed, those who recite God's Book	35:29	إِنَّ ٱلَّذِينَ يَتْلُونَ كِتَـٰبَ ٱللَّهِ
190	And were certain of Our revelations	32:24	وَكَانُوا۟ بِـَٔايَـٰتِنَا يُوقِنُونَ
191	They believed in what was brought down upon Muhammad	47:2	ءَامَنُوا۟ بِمَا نُزِّلَ عَلَىٰ مُحَمَّدٍ
192	And of the Hereafter, they are certain	31:4	وَهُم بِٱلْءَاخِرَةِ هُمْ يُوقِنُونَ
193	They strove with their money and themselves	9:88	جَـٰهَدُوا۟ بِأَمْوَٰلِهِمْ وَأَنفُسِهِمْ
194	They honour what they have been entrusted with and their oaths	70:32	هُمْ لِأَمَـٰنَـٰتِهِمْ وَعَهْدِهِمْ رَٰعُونَ
195	And they maintain their Salat	6:92	وَهُمْ عَلَىٰ صَلَاتِهِمْ يُحَافِظُونَ
196	And those who give the Zakat	23:4	وَٱلَّذِينَ هُمْ لِلزَّكَوٰةِ فَـٰعِلُونَ

197	And those who guard their private parts	23:5	وَٱلَّذِينَ هُمْ لِفُرُوجِهِمْ حَٰفِظُونَ
198	And before dawn they would ask forgiveness	51:18	وَبِٱلْأَسْحَارِ هُمْ يَسْتَغْفِرُونَ
199	And those who are patient in the face of what has afflicted them	22:35	وَٱلصَّٰبِرِينَ عَلَىٰ مَآ أَصَابَهُمْ
200	And those who do not bear false witness	25:72	وَٱلَّذِينَ لَا يَشْهَدُونَ ٱلزُّورَ
201	They guide with the truth, and with it they establish justice	7:181	يَهْدُونَ بِٱلْحَقِّ وَبِهِۦ يَعْدِلُونَ
202	They were guided to speak righteously	22:24	هُدُوٓاْ إِلَى ٱلطَّيِّبِ مِنَ ٱلْقَوْلِ
203	And they fear none but God	33:39	وَلَا يَخْشَوْنَ أَحَدًا إِلَّا ٱللَّهَ
204	So do not fear the people but fear Me	5:44	فَلَا تَخْشَوُاْ ٱلنَّاسَ وَٱخْشَوْنِ
205	Indeed, God rewards the charitable	12:88	إِنَّ ٱللَّهَ يَجْزِى ٱلْمُتَصَدِّقِينَ
206	It is those who hasten to do good deeds	23:61	أُوْلَٰٓئِكَ يُسَٰرِعُونَ فِى ٱلْخَيْرَٰتِ
207	And when they get angry, they forgive	42:37	وَإِذَا مَا غَضِبُواْ هُمْ يَغْفِرُونَ
208	The striving of those is gratefully received	17:19	أُوْلَٰٓئِكَ كَانَ سَعْيُهُم مَّشْكُورًا
209	The one who comes with the truth, then confirms it	39:33	وَٱلَّذِى جَآءَ بِٱلصِّدْقِ وَصَدَّقَ بِهِۦ
210	God will provide them with good provisions	22:58	يَرْزُقَنَّهُمُ ٱللَّهُ رِزْقًا حَسَنًا

211	Indeed, God is the best of providers	22:58	إِنَّ ٱللَّهَ لَهُوَ خَيْرُ ٱلرَّٰزِقِينَ
212	And grants a great reward from Him	4:40	وَيُؤْتِ مِن لَّدُنْهُ أَجْرًا عَظِيمًا
213	Those shall have the high ranks	20:75	أُوْلَٰٓئِكَ لَهُمُ ٱلدَّرَجَٰتُ ٱلْعُلَىٰ
214	And none attains it except the patient ones	28:80	وَلَا يُلَقَّىٰهَآ إِلَّا ٱلصَّٰبِرُونَ
215	He granted you of all that you asked Him for	14:34	ءَاتَىٰكُم مِّن كُلِّ مَا سَأَلْتُمُوهُ
216	Whoever is appreciative is appreciative for his own good	27:40	مَن شَكَرَ فَإِنَّمَا يَشْكُرُ لِنَفْسِهِ
217	As for the one who is unappreciative; indeed, my Lord is Rich, Generous	27:40	وَمَن كَفَرَ فَإِنَّ رَبِّي غَنِيٌّ كَرِيمٌ
218	The worldly life is but play and amusement	47:36	ٱلْحَيَوٰةُ ٱلدُّنْيَا لَعِبٌ وَلَهْوٌ
219	What is with God is better than any amusement	62:11	مَا عِندَ ٱللَّهِ خَيْرٌ مِّنَ ٱللَّهْوِ
220	Indeed, what is with God is better for you	16:95	إِنَّمَا عِندَ ٱللَّهِ هُوَ خَيْرٌ لَّكُمْ
221	What is at God is far better for the pious	3:198	مَا عِندَ ٱللَّهِ خَيْرٌ لِّلْأَبْرَارِ
222	Without a doubt, it is God's party who are the successful ones	58:22	إِنَّ حِزْبَ ٱللَّهِ هُمُ ٱلْمُفْلِحُونَ
223	Then indeed, it is God's party who are the victorious ones	5:56	فَإِنَّ حِزْبَ ٱللَّهِ هُمُ ٱلْغَٰلِبُونَ

224	Indeed, God is Capable of granting them victory	22:39	إِنَّ ٱللَّهَ عَلَىٰ نَصْرِهِمْ لَقَدِيرٌ
225	God replaces their bad deeds with good deeds	25:70	يُبَدِّلُ ٱللَّهُ سَيِّئَاتِهِمْ حَسَنَـٰتٍ
226	They say, "Our Lord, we have believed	3:16	يَقُولُونَ رَبَّنَآ إِنَّنَآ ءَامَنَّا
227	Those will be redeemed by God	4:17	فَأُوْلَـٰٓئِكَ يَتُوبُ ٱللَّهُ عَلَيْهِمْ
228	He will admit them by an entrance which they will be pleased with	22:59	لَيُدْخِلَنَّهُم مُّدْخَلًا يَرْضَوْنَهُ
229	Be patient, for indeed, the outcome belongs to the reverent	11:49	ٱصْبِرْ إِنَّ ٱلْعَـٰقِبَةَ لِلْمُتَّقِينَ
230	And ask Him for forgiveness. Indeed, He is Redeemer	110:3	وَٱسْتَغْفِرْهُ إِنَّهُ كَانَ تَوَّابًا

Chapter 6: The Hereafter

It is God who brings to life and puts to death. With God lies the knowledge of the "Hour" (Day of Resurrection). No person knows when or where he/she will die. The worldly life is indeed brief, then all shall be returned to their Creator.

Various physical events are detailed in the Quran regarding what will happen on the Day of Resurrection. On that Day, every self will be accountable for what it has done and no one will be wronged in any way. Every person will be given his book of deeds.

Great punishment will be assigned to those who disbelieved in God and denied His messengers. On that Day neither wealth nor children will avail the wicked. They will be thrown into the fire which they used to deny.

Those whom they used to call upon will desert them. No intercession will benefit them and they will know then that they chose the falsehood of the devil in place of God's guidance and truth. In their desperation, they will blame one another for their damnation.

Not so for God's pure servants. They shall be told "Peace be upon you. Enter Paradise." Untold blessings will be theirs in Paradise, and in eternal bliss, they shall permanently remain.

On that Day, the companions of Paradise are the triumphant ones. Indeed, this is the great triumph.

The following Quranic sentences provide a more detailed account of the above information:

The Hereafter

Following Islam is the means for redemption in the Hereafter

1	With God is the knowledge of the Hour	31:34	إِنَّ ٱللَّهَ عِندَهُۥ عِلۡمُ ٱلسَّاعَةِ
2	You are only a warner for those who fear it	79:45	إِنَّمَآ أَنتَ مُنذِرُ مَن يَخۡشَىٰهَا
3	No self knows in which land it will die	31:34	مَا تَدۡرِى نَفۡسُۢ بِأَيِّ أَرۡضٍ تَمُوتُ
4	And they are unaware as to when will they be resurrected	27:65	وَمَا يَشۡعُرُونَ أَيَّانَ يُبۡعَثُونَ
5	We belong to God and to Him we will return	2:156	إِنَّا لِلَّهِ وَإِنَّآ إِلَيۡهِ رَٰجِعُونَ
6	Indeed, to our Lord we shall return	43:14	وَإِنَّآ إِلَىٰ رَبِّنَا لَمُنقَلِبُونَ
7	God is the Ally, and He brings the dead to life	42:9	هُوَ ٱلۡوَلِىُّ وَهُوَ يُحۡى ٱلۡمَوۡتَىٰ
8	It is upon Him to bring about the other creation	53:47	وَأَنَّ عَلَيۡهِ ٱلنَّشۡأَةَ ٱلۡأُخۡرَىٰ
9	Just as We initiated the first creation, We shall repeat it	21:104	كَمَا بَدَأۡنَآ أَوَّلَ خَلۡقٍ نُّعِيدُهُۥ
10	Then they are returned to God, their true Master	6:62	ثُمَّ رُدُّوٓاْ إِلَى ٱللَّهِ مَوۡلَىٰهُمُ
11	They are brought forward before God; the One, the All-Conquering	14:48	بَرَزُواْ لِلَّهِ ٱلۡوَٰحِدِ ٱلۡقَهَّارِ
12	Indeed, to Us belongs the Hereafter and the first life	92:13	إِنَّ لَنَا لَلۡءَاخِرَةَ وَٱلۡأُولَىٰ

13	When the great calamity arrives	79:34	إِذَا جَاءَتِ ٱلطَّامَّةُ ٱلْكُبْرَىٰ
14	And the trance of death came with the truth	50:19	وَجَاءَتْ سَكْرَةُ ٱلْمَوْتِ بِٱلْحَقِّ
15	Why then, if you are not guilty	56:86	فَلَوْلَا إِن كُنتُمْ غَيْرَ مَدِينِينَ
16	Do you wish to send it back if you are truthful?	56:87	تَرْجِعُونَهَا إِن كُنتُمْ صَادِقِينَ
17	There is no self that has no guardian over it	86:4	إِن كُلُّ نَفْسٍ لَّمَّا عَلَيْهَا حَافِظٌ
18	On the Day of Resurrection, you will surely be resurrected	23:16	إِنَّكُمْ يَوْمَ ٱلْقِيَامَةِ تُبْعَثُونَ
19	He will inform you of what you used to do	62:8	يُنَبِّئُكُم بِمَا كُنتُمْ تَعْمَلُونَ
20	The Day when the earth and the mountains will shake	73:14	يَوْمَ تَرْجُفُ ٱلْأَرْضُ وَٱلْجِبَالُ
21	On the Day the sky will split open with clouds	25:25	يَوْمَ تَشَقَّقُ ٱلسَّمَاءُ بِٱلْغَمَامِ
22	The Day when the sky will be like molten brass	70:8	يَوْمَ تَكُونُ ٱلسَّمَاءُ كَٱلْمُهْلِ
23	And your Lord comes, with the angels, row after row	89:22	وَجَاءَ رَبُّكَ وَٱلْمَلَكُ صَفًّا صَفًّا
24	The faces were humbled before the Living, the Eternal	20:111	عَنَتِ ٱلْوُجُوهُ لِلْحَيِّ ٱلْقَيُّومِ
25	And the earth shone with the Light of its Lord	39:69	وَأَشْرَقَتِ ٱلْأَرْضُ بِنُورِ رَبِّهَا
26	The Day We raise from every nation a witness	16:84	يَوْمَ نَبْعَثُ مِن كُلِّ أُمَّةٍ شَهِيدًا

27	The prophets and the witnesses were brought forth	39:69	جِاْىٓءَ بِٱلنَّبِيِّـۧنَ وَٱلشُّهَدَآءِ
28	So today, no self will be wronged in any way	36:54	فَٱلْيَوْمَ لَا تُظْلَمُ نَفْسٌ شَيْـًٔا
29	Our Book utters the truth about you	45:29	كِتَـٰبُنَا يَنطِقُ عَلَيْكُم بِٱلْحَقِّ
30	Indeed, their Lord is All-Aware of them on that Day?	100:11	إِنَّ رَبَّهُم بِهِمْ يَوْمَئِذٍ لَّخَبِيرٌ
31	Then, how would you know what the Day of the Religion is?	82:18	ثُمَّ مَآ أَدْرَىٰكَ مَا يَوْمُ ٱلدِّينِ
32	The Day when the human being will remember all his striving	79:35	يَوْمَ يَتَذَكَّرُ ٱلْإِنسَـٰنُ مَا سَعَىٰ
33	So for the one who is given his book in his right hand	69:19	أَمَّا مَنْ أُوتِىَ كِتَـٰبَهُۥ بِيَمِينِهِ
34	He will be given an easy reckoning	84:8	فَسَوْفَ يُحَاسَبُ حِسَابًا يَسِيرًا
35	And will return to his family joyfully	84:9	وَيَنقَلِبُ إِلَىٰٓ أَهْلِهِۦ مَسْرُورًا
36	He will say, "Here, read my book"	69:19	يَقُولُ هَآؤُمُ ٱقْرَءُوا۟ كِتَـٰبِيَهْ
37	I certainly knew that I was going to receive my reckoning	69:20	إِنِّى ظَنَنتُ أَنِّى مُلَـٰقٍ حِسَابِيَهْ
38	He will admit them into Paradise which He has made known to them	47:6	يُدْخِلُهُمُ ٱلْجَنَّةَ عَرَّفَهَا لَهُمْ
39	A high Garden with its ripe fruits hanging low	69:22-23	جَنَّةٍ عَالِيَةٍ قُطُوفُهَا دَانِيَةٌ

40	As for the one who is given his book in his left hand	69:25	أَمَّا مَنْ أُوتِيَ كِتَٰبَهُۥ بِشِمَالِهِ
41	He will have no share in the Hereafter	42:20	مَا لَهُۥ فِى ٱلْءَاخِرَةِ مِن نَّصِيبٍ
42	So he has no friend here today	69:35	فَلَيْسَ لَهُ ٱلْيَوْمَ هَٰهُنَا حَمِيمٌ
43	The Day We strike the great strike	44:16	يَوْمَ نَبْطِشُ ٱلْبَطْشَةَ ٱلْكُبْرَىٰ
44	The Day when the transgressor will bite his hands	25:27	يَوْمَ يَعَضُّ ٱلظَّالِمُ عَلَىٰ يَدَيْهِ
45	There will be no good news for the criminals that Day	25:22	لَا بُشْرَىٰ يَوْمَئِذٍ لِّلْمُجْرِمِينَ
46	We have sent warners in their midst	37:72	لَقَدْ أَرْسَلْنَا فِيهِم مُّنذِرِينَ
47	But the transgressors refuse everything except disbelief	17:99	فَأَبَى ٱلظَّٰلِمُونَ إِلَّا كُفُورًا
48	And those before them have denied	67:18	وَلَقَدْ كَذَّبَ ٱلَّذِينَ مِن قَبْلِهِمْ
49	Indeed, We found most of them to be wicked	7:102	إِن وَجَدْنَآ أَكْثَرَهُمْ لَفَٰسِقِينَ
50	A messenger had come to them from amongst themselves, but they denied him	16:113	جَآءَهُمْ رَسُولٌ مِّنْهُمْ فَكَذَّبُوهُ
51	We are disbelievers in what you have been sent with	43:24	إِنَّا بِمَآ أُرْسِلْتُم بِهِۦ كَٰفِرُونَ
52	And they used to reject Our revelations	41:15	وَكَانُواْ بِـَٔايَٰتِنَا يَجْحَدُونَ

53	So they were struck by the ill effects of what they had done	16:34	فَأَصَابَهُمْ سَيِّئَاتُ مَا عَمِلُواْ
54	Miserable indeed is what their selves brought forth upon them	5:80	لَبِئْسَ مَا قَدَّمَتْ لَهُمْ أَنفُسُهُمْ
55	How will it be when the angels take them back	47:27	كَيْفَ إِذَا تَوَفَّتْهُمُ ٱلْمَلَـٰٓئِكَةُ
56	Beating their faces and their hinds	47:27	يَضْرِبُونَ وُجُوهَهُمْ وَأَدْبَـٰرَهُمْ
57	They will be arraigned unto the punishment	30:16	أُوْلَـٰٓئِكَ فِى ٱلْعَذَابِ مُحْضَرُونَ
58	The punishment struck them while they were transgressing	16:113	أَخَذَهُمُ ٱلْعَذَابُ وَهُمْ ظَـٰلِمُونَ
59	On that Day, they will be partitioned from their Lord	83:15	عَن رَّبِّهِمْ يَوْمَئِذٍ لَّمَحْجُوبُونَ
60	The Day when neither wealth nor children can be of any benefit	26:88	يَوْمَ لَا يَنفَعُ مَالٌ وَلَا بَنُونَ
61	The Day when they are tormented over the Fire	51:13	يَوْمَ هُمْ عَلَى ٱلنَّارِ يُفْتَنُونَ
62	We will say, "Taste the punishment of the Fire	3:181	نَقُولُ ذُوقُواْ عَذَابَ ٱلْحَرِيقِ
63	This is what you used to doubt	44:50	إِنَّ هَـٰذَا مَا كُنتُم بِهِۦ تَمْتَرُونَ
64	So they were struck by the ill effects of what they had earned	39:51	فَأَصَابَهُمْ سَيِّئَاتُ مَا كَسَبُواْ
65	So that He may question the truthful about their truthfulness	33:8	لِيَسْـَٔلَ ٱلصَّـٰدِقِينَ عَن صِدْقِهِمْ

66	The Day when the truthful will benefit from their truthfulness	5:119	يَوْمُ يَنفَعُ ٱلصَّـٰدِقِينَ صِدْقُهُمْ
67	As for those whose faces are blackened	3:106	أَمَّا ٱلَّذِينَ ٱسْوَدَّتْ وُجُوهُهُمْ
68	Who harbour bad thoughts about God	48:6	ٱلظَّآنِّينَ بِٱللَّهِ ظَنَّ ٱلسَّوْءِ
69	And God is angry with them and He cursed them	48:6	وَغَضِبَ ٱللَّهُ عَلَيْهِمْ وَلَعَنَهُمْ
70	Their schemes will not avail them in any way	52:46	لَا يُغْنِى عَنْهُمْ كَيْدُهُمْ شَيْـًٔا
71	And they assigned to Him a share of His own servants	43:15	وَجَعَلُواْ لَهُۥ مِنْ عِبَادِهِۦ جُزْءًا
72	He will let them taste the consequences of some of what they had done	30:41	لِيُذِيقَهُم بَعْضَ ٱلَّذِى عَمِلُواْ
73	And as for those whose faces are whitened	3:107	وَأَمَّا ٱلَّذِينَ ٱبْيَضَّتْ وُجُوهُهُمْ
74	The angels take them back in a state of righteousness	16:32	تَتَوَفَّىٰهُمُ ٱلْمَلَـٰٓئِكَةُ طَيِّبِينَ
75	Peace be upon you. Enter paradise	16:32	سَلَـٰمٌ عَلَيْكُمُ ٱدْخُلُواْ ٱلْجَنَّةَ
76	Therein, they shall permanently remain. God's promise is truthful	31:9	خَـٰلِدِينَ فِيهَا وَعْدَ ٱللَّهِ حَقًّا
77	That is a great triumph with God	48:5	ذَٰلِكَ عِندَ ٱللَّهِ فَوْزًا عَظِيمًا
78	God shielded them from the evil of that Day	76:11	وَقَىٰهُمُ ٱللَّهُ شَرَّ ذَٰلِكَ ٱلْيَوْمِ

79	And they are secure from the horrors of that Day	27:89	وَهُم مِّن فَزَعٍ يَوْمَئِذٍ ءَامِنُونَ
80	He will summon them. He is Wise, Knowledgeable	15:25	هُوَ يَحْشُرُهُمْ إِنَّهُۥ حَكِيمٌ عَلِيمٌ
81	God issues the judgment and none can reverse His Judgment	13:41	ٱللَّهُ يَحْكُمُ لَا مُعَقِّبَ لِحُكْمِهِ
82	Judgement belongs to God, the Most High, the Great	40:12	ٱلْحُكْمُ لِلَّهِ ٱلْعَلِيِّ ٱلْكَبِيرِ
83	The matter is up to God, both before and after	30:4	لِلَّهِ ٱلْأَمْرُ مِن قَبْلُ وَمِنْ بَعْدُ
84	Such is that, while the transgressors shall have the worst homecoming	38:55	هَٰذَا وَإِنَّ لِلطَّٰغِينَ لَشَرَّ مَعَابٍ
85	And indeed, it is a cause of remorse for the disbelievers	69:50	وَإِنَّهُۥ لَحَسْرَةٌ عَلَى ٱلْكَٰفِرِينَ
86	And the ill effects of what they had done became apparent to them	45:33	وَبَدَا لَهُمْ سَيِّـَٔاتُ مَا عَمِلُواْ
87	And the ill effects of what they had earned became apparent to them	39:48	وَبَدَا لَهُمْ سَيِّـَٔاتُ مَا كَسَبُواْ
88	So God's curse is on the disbelievers	2:89	فَلَعْنَةُ ٱللَّهِ عَلَى ٱلْكَٰفِرِينَ
89	The gates of heaven will not open for them	7:40	لَا تُفَتَّحُ لَهُمْ أَبْوَٰبُ ٱلسَّمَآءِ
90	Those are the depraved disbelievers	80:42	أُوْلَٰٓئِكَ هُمُ ٱلْكَفَرَةُ ٱلْفَجَرَةُ
91	They had no protector against God	40:21	مَا كَانَ لَهُم مِّنَ ٱللَّهِ مِن وَاقٍ

92	If you could see when they are made to stand before their Lord	6:30	لَوْ تَرَىٰٓ إِذْ وُقِفُواْ عَلَىٰ رَبِّهِمْ
93	They hang down their heads before their Lord	32:12	نَاكِسُواْ رُءُوسِهِمْ عِندَ رَبِّهِمْ
94	With their eyesight subdued, humiliation will overwhelm them	68:43	خَٰشِعَةً أَبْصَٰرُهُمْ تَرْهَقُهُمْ ذِلَّةٌ
95	On the Day He calls out to them, "Where are My partners?"	41:47	يَوْمَ يُنَادِيهِمْ أَيْنَ شُرَكَآءِى
96	That which they used to fabricate has deserted them	16:87	ضَلَّ عَنْهُم مَّا كَانُواْ يَفْتَرُونَ
97	And those whom they used to call upon before deserted them	41:48	وَضَلَّ عَنْهُم مَّا كَانُواْ يَدْعُونَ
98	And will totally reject their worship	46:6	وَكَانُواْ بِعِبَادَتِهِمْ كَٰفِرِينَ
99	And so, they renounced their partners	30:13	وَكَانُواْ بِشُرَكَآئِهِمْ كَٰفِرِينَ
100	If the Almighty willed, we would not have worshipped them	43:20	لَوْ شَآءَ ٱلرَّحْمَٰنُ مَا عَبَدْنَٰهُم
101	And God bears witness that they are liars	9:107	وَٱللَّهُ يَشْهَدُ إِنَّهُمْ لَكَٰذِبُونَ
102	God will pay them their rightful due in full	24:25	يُوَفِّيهِمُ ٱللَّهُ دِينَهُمُ ٱلْحَقَّ
103	And they will know that God is the Truth	24:25	وَيَعْلَمُونَ أَنَّ ٱللَّهَ هُوَ ٱلْحَقُّ

104	On that Day, none will punish as His punishment	89:25	يَوْمَئِذٍ لَّا يُعَذِّبُ عَذَابَهُۥٓ أَحَدٌ
105	We do not delay it except to an already counted term	11:104	مَا نُؤَخِّرُهُۥٓ إِلَّا لِأَجَلٍ مَّعْدُودٍ
106	We will gather them around Hell on their knees	19:68	لَنُحْضِرَنَّهُمْ حَوْلَ جَهَنَّمَ جِثِيًّا
107	To be seized by the forelocks and the feet	55:41	يُؤْخَذُ بِٱلنَّوَٰصِى وَٱلْأَقْدَامِ
108	Indeed, We have shackles and Hellfire	73:12	إِنَّ لَدَيْنَآ أَنكَالًا وَجَحِيمًا
109	Hell is the appointed place for all of them	15:43	إِنَّ جَهَنَّمَ لَمَوْعِدُهُمْ أَجْمَعِينَ
110	They were thrown into it headfirst, they and the strayers	26:94	كُبْكِبُوا۟ فِيهَا هُمْ وَٱلْغَاوُۥنَ
111	They will hear it raging and fuming	25:12	سَمِعُوا۟ لَهَا تَغَيُّظًا وَزَفِيرًا
112	And its punishment will not be lightened for them	35:36	وَلَا يُخَفَّفُ عَنْهُم مِّنْ عَذَابِهَا
113	We will add more punishment to their punishment	16:88	زِدْنَٰهُمْ عَذَابًا فَوْقَ ٱلْعَذَابِ
114	A hospitality of boiling water, and a roasting in Hellfire	56:93-94	نُزُلٌ مِّنْ حَمِيمٍ وَتَصْلِيَةُ جَحِيمٍ
115	They will have no food except from a thorny plant	88:6	لَّيْسَ لَهُمْ طَعَامٌ إِلَّا مِن ضَرِيعٍ
116	This is what you used to deny	83:17	هَٰذَا ٱلَّذِى كُنتُم بِهِۦ تُكَذِّبُونَ

117	You used to shun His revelations arrogantly	6:93	كُنتُمْ عَنْ ءَايَتِهِۦ تَسْتَكْبِرُونَ
118	And that which you used to claim has deserted you	6:94	وَضَلَّ عَنكُم مَّا كُنتُمْ تَزْعُمُونَ
119	Likewise did those before them deny	6:148	كَذَٰلِكَ كَذَّبَ ٱلَّذِينَ مِن قَبْلِهِم
120	And God knows that they are liars	9:42	وَٱللَّهُ يَعْلَمُ إِنَّهُمْ لَكَٰذِبُونَ
121	The intercession of the intercessors will not avail them	74:48	مَا تَنفَعُهُمْ شَفَٰعَةُ ٱلشَّٰفِعِينَ
122	The hypocrites are indeed the wicked ones	9:67	إِنَّ ٱلْمُنَٰفِقِينَ هُمُ ٱلْفَٰسِقُونَ
123	Those are the ones whom God has cursed	4:52	أُوْلَٰئِكَ ٱلَّذِينَ لَعَنَهُمُ ٱللَّهُ
124	Satan has indeed confirmed his thoughts about them to be true	34:20	لَقَدْ صَدَّقَ عَلَيْهِمْ إِبْلِيسُ ظَنَّهُ
125	He has misguided great multitudes of you	36:62	لَقَدْ أَضَلَّ مِنكُمْ جِبِلًّا كَثِيرًا
126	Enter the Fire with those who are entering	66:10	ٱدْخُلَا ٱلنَّارَ مَعَ ٱلدَّٰخِلِينَ
127	You are sharing in the punishment	43:39	أَنَّكُمْ فِى ٱلْعَذَابِ مُشْتَرِكُونَ
128	The messengers of our Lord had come with the truth	7:43	لَقَدْ جَآءَتْ رُسُلُ رَبِّنَا بِٱلْحَقِّ
129	Our Lord, our misery got the better of us	23:106	رَبَّنَا غَلَبَتْ عَلَيْنَا شِقْوَتُنَا
130	Glory to our Lord! Indeed, we have been transgressors	68:29	سُبْحَٰنَ رَبِّنَآ إِنَّا كُنَّا ظَٰلِمِينَ

131	None misled us other than the criminals	26:99	وَمَآ أَضَلَّنَآ إِلَّا ٱلۡمُجۡرِمُونَ
132	The Word has been rightly deserved upon the majority of them	36:7	لَقَدۡ حَقَّ ٱلۡقَوۡلُ عَلَىٰٓ أَكۡثَرِهِمۡ
133	Today no ransom shall be accepted from you	57:15	ٱلۡيَوۡمَ لَا يُؤۡخَذُ مِنكُمۡ فِدۡيَةٌ
134	Your refuge is the Fire; it is your master	57:15	مَأۡوَىٰكُمُ ٱلنَّارُ هِىَ مَوۡلَىٰكُمۡ
135	Remain despised therein and do not speak to Me	23:108	ٱخۡسَـُٔواْ فِيهَا وَلَا تُكَلِّمُونِ
136	Today you are repaid with the punishment of humiliation	46:20	ٱلۡيَوۡمَ تُجۡزَوۡنَ عَذَابَ ٱلۡهُونِ
137	Not so for God's pure servants	37:40	إِلَّا عِبَادَ ٱللَّهِ ٱلۡمُخۡلَصِينَ
138	They receive good news of a blessing from God	3:171	يَسۡتَبۡشِرُونَ بِنِعۡمَةٍ مِّنَ ٱللَّهِ
139	A better place of settlement and better haven	25:24	خَيۡرٌ مُّسۡتَقَرًّا وَأَحۡسَنُ مَقِيلًا
140	None attains it except those with extremely good fortune	41:35	مَا يُلَقَّىٰهَآ إِلَّا ذُو حَظٍّ عَظِيمٍ
141	The greatest horror will not grieve them	21:103	لَا يَحۡزُنُهُمُ ٱلۡفَزَعُ ٱلۡأَكۡبَرُ
142	God will save those who were reverent	39:61	وَيُنَجِّى ٱللَّهُ ٱلَّذِينَ ٱتَّقَوۡاْ
143	We stripped away what animosity there was from their chests	15:47	نَزَعۡنَا مَا فِى صُدُورِهِم مِّنۡ غِلٍّ

144	Those will be rewarded with the mansions in return for their patience	25:75	يُجْزَوْنَ ٱلْغُرْفَةَ بِمَا صَبَرُواْ
145	And therein they will be received with greetings and with peace	25:75	وَيُلَقَّوْنَ فِيهَا تَحِيَّةً وَسَلَـٰمًا
146	And for those who feared the position of their Lord are two Gardens	55:46	وَلِمَنْ خَافَ مَقَامَ رَبِّهِۦ جَنَّتَانِ
147	And those who have responded to their Lord	42:38	وَٱلَّذِينَ ٱسْتَجَابُواْ لِرَبِّهِمْ
148	Their Lord has shielded them from the punishment of Hellfire	52:18	وَقَىٰهُمْ رَبُّهُمْ عَذَابَ ٱلْجَحِيمِ
149	It is binding on Us to save the believers	10:103	حَقًّا عَلَيْنَا نُنجِ ٱلْمُؤْمِنِينَ
150	It is a promise that is binding upon your Lord	25:16	كَانَ عَلَىٰ رَبِّكَ وَعْدًا مَّسْـُٔولًا
151	We have found what our Lord promised us to be true	7:44	وَجَدْنَا مَا وَعَدَنَا رَبُّنَا حَقًّا
152	We settle in Paradise wherever we may please	39:74	نَتَبَوَّأُ مِنَ ٱلْجَنَّةِ حَيْثُ نَشَآءُ
153	Thus does God reward the reverent	16:31	كَذَٰلِكَ يَجْزِى ٱللَّهُ ٱلْمُتَّقِينَ
154	Indeed, the reverent will be in a secure place	44:51	إِنَّ ٱلْمُتَّقِينَ فِى مَقَامٍ أَمِينٍ
155	Indeed, the reverent are in gardens and bliss	52:17	إِنَّ ٱلْمُتَّقِينَ فِى جَنَّـٰتٍ وَنَعِيمٍ
156	Indeed, the reverent will be in gardens and springs	51:15	إِنَّ ٱلْمُتَّقِينَ فِى جَنَّـٰتٍ وَعُيُونٍ

157	Indeed, the reverent will be amid shades and springs	77:41	إِنَّ ٱلْمُتَّقِينَ فِى ظِلَـٰلٍ وَعُيُونٍ
158	And Gardens wherein they are granted everlasting bliss	9:21	وَجَنَّـٰتٍ لَّهُمْ فِيهَا نَعِيمٌ مُّقِيمٌ
159	They shall be amid thornless lote-trees, and clustered banana trees	56:28-29	فِى سِدْرٍ مَّخْضُودٍ وَطَلْحٍ مَّنضُودٍ
160	And poured water, and plenty of fruits	56:31-32	وَمَآءٍ مَّسْكُوبٍ وَفَـٰكِهَةٍ كَثِيرَةٍ
161	Grains with husks, and fragrant herbs	55:12	ٱلْحَبُّ ذُو ٱلْعَصْفِ وَٱلرَّيْحَانُ
162	Passing by them will be immortal boys	56:17	يَطُوفُ عَلَيْهِمْ وِلْدَٰنٌ مُّخَلَّدُونَ
163	Golden trays and cups will be passed among them	43:71	يُطَافُ عَلَيْهِم بِصِحَافٍ مِّن ذَهَبٍ
164	Therein is what the self desires	43:71	وَفِيهَا مَا تَشْتَهِيهِ ٱلْأَنفُسُ
165	In it there is a spring called 'Salsabeel'	76:18	عَيْنًا فِيهَا تُسَمَّىٰ سَلْسَبِيلًا
166	A spring from which the servants of God will drink	76:6	عَيْنًا يَشْرَبُ بِهَا عِبَادُ ٱللَّهِ
167	A spring from which those brought near will drink	83:28	عَيْنًا يَشْرَبُ بِهَا ٱلْمُقَرَّبُونَ
168	A cup from a flowing spring will be passed among them	37:45	يُطَافُ عَلَيْهِم بِكَأْسٍ مِّن مَّعِينٍ
169	They are given pure drinks by their Lord	76:21	سَقَىٰهُمْ رَبُّهُمْ شَرَابًا طَهُورًا
170	Rivers of wine that is a pleasure for the drinkers	47:15	أَنْهَـٰرٌ مِّنْ خَمْرٍ لَّذَّةٍ لِّلشَّـٰرِبِينَ

171	There with them shall be maidens of same-age and with subdued glances	38:52	عِندَهُمْ قَصِرَتُ ٱلطَّرْفِ أَتْرَابٌ
172	Such is Our provision which will never run out	38:54	هَذَا لَرِزْقُنَا مَا لَهُ مِن نَّفَادٍ
173	Indeed, We thus reward the good-doers	37:121	إِنَّا كَذَلِكَ نَجْزِى ٱلْمُحْسِنِينَ
174	God is pleased with them and they are pleased with Him	58:22	رَضِيَ ٱللَّهُ عَنْهُمْ وَرَضُواْ عَنْهُ
175	The companions of Paradise are the triumphant	59:20	أَصْحَبُ ٱلْجَنَّةِ هُمُ ٱلْفَآئِزُونَ
176	Indeed, this is the great triumph	37:60	إِنَّ هَذَا لَهُوَ ٱلْفَوْزُ ٱلْعَظِيمُ

Chapter 7: The Design

From the tables above we have the following data:

Number of sentences

God	149
Messenger	48
Quran	30
Islam	230
Hereafter	176
	633

Now that we have read all the above sentences and seen how they deliver a comprehensive summary of the Quranic message, we need to ask: What do all these sentences have in common? Is there any special design in them that makes them a true sign from God, or are they merely random sentences placed in a sequence that makes sense?

Every one of the above sentences
(total 633) consists of 19 Arabic Letters

What we are seeing here is a deliberate design that employs the number 19 to produce an awesome pattern that speaks to us and spells out the full Quranic message in clear words!

Every one of the 633 sentences above is an integral part of the message of the Quran and every sentence is used as it appears in the Quran and without any alterations.

Why 19?

The mathematical coding of the Quran with the number 19 makes one wonder about the divine reason for choosing the number 19 instead of some other number. Why not 17 or 23 or any other random number?

First

Number 19 is the numerical value of the Arabic word WAHD (One).

WAHD (pronounced Wahed) is one of the principal Names of God. The Arabic word WAHD consists of 4 Arabic letters: W,A,H,D.

In the past, before the invention of the number system (1 to 9), all peoples of the world used the letters of their alphabets as numbers. As an example, we witness the remains of this use in Roman numerals where X=10 and V=5 and so on.

The Arabs also used the letters of their alphabet as numbers. The numerical values of the Arabic letters are derived from what is known as the 'abjaddiyah'. This arrangement of the Arabic alphabet dates back to at least 700 BC.

The 'abjaddiyah' arrangement of the Arabic letters is still in use today, particularly in legal documents and law.

The numerical values of the letters W, A, H, D are 6, 1, 8, and 4, respectively.

These numbers add up to 19 (6 + 1 + 8 + 4 = 19).

The number 19 can therefore be considered a representation of the First Commandment in all divine Scriptures; that there is only ONE God.

Second

Number 19 comprises the numerals: 1 and 9. These are the first and last (single) numerals used in mathematics. Number 19 represents the First and Last or the Alpha and Omega. These are attributes of God as confirmed in the Scriptures.

He is the First and the Last, the External and the Internal, and He is Knowledgeable of all things. (Quran 57:3)

I am the Alpha and the Omega, the First and the Last, the Beginning and the End. (Bible, Revelations 22:13)

It is also worth mentioning that the numbers 1 and 9 are the only two numbers that look the same in Arabic, Hebrew and all Western languages (English, Spanish, French, etc.)

Chapter 8: The Analysis

1- The instructions and commands of God in the Quran are extensive. The above list of sentences provides only a summary of the message of the Book, albeit a comprehensive summary. It is therefore natural that the sentences above do not cover every instruction and detail found in the Quran. The Quranic instructions that do not show on the list above are nevertheless covered by the following 19-lettered sentence:

Say "Obey God and the messenger"	3:32	قُلْ أَطِيعُوا۟ ٱللَّهَ وَٱلرَّسُولَ

Obeying God and His messenger requires the believers to obey each one of the individual instructions, commands, rules and laws laid down by God in the Quran. Ultimately, the 19-lettered sentence above (3:32) covers every instruction or law that is not present in the comprehensive summary.

2- It must also be noted that the above sentences are not the only 19-lettered sentences to be found in the Quran. The Quran contains numerous other 19-lettered sentences that were not included in the list. The reason being any of the following:

a- Sentences that are repetitions, either in words or in meaning, of sentences that are already on the list.

b- Sentences that contain narrative information which, although of demonstrative or reflective value, is related to a specific people or time rather than being components of the universal message of the Quran that is addressed to all people and at all times.

Example

Moses came to you with clear proofs	2:92	لَقَدْ جَآءَكُم مُّوسَىٰ بِٱلْبَيِّنَٰتِ

The sentence above is addressed specifically to the people of Moses. The same message when addressed to all mankind is found in the following 19-lettered sentence which is already on our list (see 'The Messenger' list):

And their messengers came to them with the clear proofs	10:13	وَجَآءَتْهُمْ رُسُلُهُم بِٱلْبَيِّنَٰتِ

When 10:13 is quoted, it covers the clear proofs brought by any messenger.

c- We also find Quranic sentences that are formed of 19 letters but they could not be quoted in isolation from the rest of the verse they came from. If they are quoted in isolation, they would portray an incomplete or even incorrect meaning. And since every one of the above sentences is a complete message, it would be inappropriate to include that category of sentences in the list. The following is one example:

| He multiplies it manifold for him | 2:245 | فَيُضَٰعِفَهُۥ لَهُۥٓ أَضْعَافًا كَثِيرَةً |

This may appear to be a complete sentence, however, the correct meaning can only be attained when we read the complete verse. The complete meaning of the verse is:

"For the one who lends God a good loan, God will multiply it manifold for him."

Therefore, the 19-lettered sentence in 2:245 cannot be included in our list.

Another example of a 19-lettered sentence that cannot be included in the list for the same reason (not a complete sentence) is:

| The one who fabricates lies about God | 3:94 | مَنِ ٱفْتَرَىٰ عَلَى ٱللَّهِ ٱلْكَذِبَ |

3- The Quran places special emphasis on the prohibition of ascribing partners to God or associating anything or anyone with Him (shirk). It also emphasises the importance of observing the Salat and giving the Zakat. Surely enough, we find various 19-lettered sentences that address these aspects of the religion, such as the 19-lettered phrases found in 6:92, 22:31, 23:4 and 30:31.

As mentioned, the Quran does not contain 19-lettered sentences that cover every instruction or ritual of the religion. Nevertheless, it is important to stress again that all such commands are covered under the 19-lettered sentence that contains the command to obey God and the messenger.

4- Some may rightly wonder why some letters have been dropped at the beginning of some of the original Arabic Quranic sentences. An example is the following sentence:

| Which of your Lord's favours do you deny | 55:18 | بِأَيِّ ءَالَآءِ رَبِّكُمَا تُكَذِّبَانِ |

The full Arabic verse has the letter (f) at the beginning of the first word, which translates to (so) in English. The letter (f) makes the sentence:

So in which of your Lord's favours do you deny	55:18	فَبِأَيّ ءَالَآءِ رَبِّكُمَا تُكَذِّبَانِ

The Arabic letters (b), (f), and (w), even though are single letters found at the beginning of various Arabic words, they are in fact <u>separate words</u>. When these letters are translated into English, they appear as independent words.

The letter (b) translates to (with)

The letter (f) translates to (then/so)

The letter (w) translates to (and/also).

We must always be focused on the fact that we are looking for Quranic sentences which are <u>complete in meaning</u>. They do not have to be complete verses. In such cases where some of these Arabic letters are dropped, we would not be dropping letters from existing words, we would be dropping <u>whole words</u>. What is important is that when such letters are dropped, we still end up with complete sentences.

It must also be said that these letters only contribute to the meaning when the preceding words/verses are read. But when we are reading the 19-lettered sentences above on their own, independently of the complete verses, the unused letters do not alter or change the message in the sentences. Thus, it is perfectly acceptable to use these sentences with or without the letters mentioned because in both cases they provide complete and independent messages.

In our example of 55:18, using the sentence without the letter (f), which means (so), we still get a sentence with a complete meaning which is:

"Which of your Lord's favours do you deny?"

When we read the verses before 55:18 we realise that God is giving us examples of many of His signs and marvels. This is then followed by the words, "So which of your Lord's favours do you deny?" The letter (f) which means (so) can only be relevant when we read the preceding verses and then read 55:18. But if we are reading our 19-lettered sentence (from 55:18) on its own (as in our list above), without the benefit of the preceding verses, it is acceptable to quote the sentence without the letter (f) since it provides a complete and independent meaning.

Chapter 9: The Challenge

A challenge is presented here to any reader who doubts the deliberate nature of this design. Some may interpret the pattern above as being coincidental! This may be the case if we were dealing with only a handful of sentences consisting of 19 letters or any fixed number, but when we have such a vast number of sentences, all composed of 19 letters and covering the overall Quranic message, this cannot be coincidental.

To verify this matter, the reader is invited to come up with an alternative set of Quranic sentences, all containing the same number of letters (other than 19). Every sentence in the set must be a complete sentence and together they must present a complete and comprehensive summary of the message of the Quran. The reader can select sentences that are composed of 15, 18, 21 or any number of letters that he chooses, and then see how far he gets.

Without a doubt, it is possible to find various Quranic sentences, each made of the same chosen number of letters (other than 19), which will cover some Quranic topics, <u>but it is impossible to compile a complete set of sentences that covers the full Quranic message by using any number other than 19.</u>

Why is it impossible?

For a start, many of these very significant 19-lettered Quranic sentences, which are integral to the Quranic message as a whole, appear in the Quran <u>only once</u>. As a result, it is not possible to find these sentences in any other Quranic verses, let alone in a different number of letters.

The following 19-lettered sentences are some examples of such sentences that appear in the Quran only once, the message of these sentences is not found in other Quranic sentences:

Who forgives the sins except for God?	3:135	مَن يَغْفِرُ ٱلذُّنُوبَ إِلَّا ٱللَّهُ
We have brought it down as an Arabic Quran	12:2	إِنَّآ أَنزَلْنَٰهُ قُرْءَٰنًا عَرَبِيًّا
Say "The Holy Ruh has brought it down from your Lord"	16:102	قُلْ نَزَّلَهُۥ رُوحُ ٱلْقُدُسِ مِن رَّبِّكَ

The Word of your Lord has been completed, in truth and justice	6:115	تَمَّتْ كَلِمَتُ رَبِّكَ صِدْقًا وَعَدْلًا
The messenger of God and the seal of the prophets	33:40	رَّسُولَ ٱللَّهِ وَخَاتَمَ ٱلنَّبِيِّيْنَ
God has selected the religion for you	2:132	إِنَّ ٱللَّهَ ٱصْطَفَىٰ لَكُمُ ٱلدِّينَ
Whatever blessing you have, it is from God	16:53	وَمَا بِكُم مِّن نِّعْمَةٍ فَمِنَ ٱللَّهِ
The human being has nothing to count for him except his own work	53:39	أَن لَّيْسَ لِلْإِنسَـٰنِ إِلَّا مَا سَعَىٰ
No self knows in which land it will die	31:34	مَا تَدْرِى نَفْسٌ بِأَىِّ أَرْضٍ تَمُوتُ
We belong to God and to Him we will return	2:156	إِنَّا لِلَّهِ وَإِنَّآ إِلَيْهِ رَٰجِعُونَ
Our Book utters the truth about you	45:29	كِتَـٰبُنَا يَنطِقُ عَلَيْكُم بِٱلْحَقِّ
Satan has indeed confirmed his thoughts about them to be true	34:20	لَقَدْ صَدَّقَ عَلَيْهِمْ إِبْلِيسُ ظَنَّهُ
It is binding on Us to save the believers	10:103	حَقًّا عَلَيْنَا نُنجِ ٱلْمُؤْمِنِينَ

The message found in each one of the above verses appears <u>only once</u> in all the Quran and it is worded in 19 letters. Every one of these 19-lettered sentences is an integral component of the overall Quranic message.

Conclusion

On witnessing this awesome design, one can only marvel at God's signs that are revealed to us. Naturally, this awesome 19-lettered design does not cover every detail in the Quran. The design for example does not include sentences about marriage or inheritance, nor many other details of the religion. To cover all the details we would need the complete Quran and not a summary.

Besides the profound role of the number 19 in other features of the Quran, what we witness in this design is a different role for code 19. In this design, we witness how God employed the number 19 to spell out the comprehensive Quranic message, thus confirming once again that the Quran is a numerically structured book.

Additionally, the fact that these 19-lettered Quranic sentences were extracted from different parts of the Quran goes a long way in confirming that the Quran, represented by these sentences, has been intact across the ages. Had the Quran been subject to corruption, we would not have found the Quranic message so comprehensively represented in sentences which are all composed of 19 Arabic letters.

<u>Praise God, the One, the Almighty</u>

Printed in Great Britain
by Amazon

32837552R00040